The Thomson Handbook Workbook

Mary Wright
Christopher Newport University

THOMSON

WADSWORTH

Australia • Brazil • Canada • Mexico • Singapore • Spain • United Kingdom • United States

The Thomson Handbook Workbook
The Thomson Handbook
David Blakesley/Jeffrey L. Hoogeveen
Prepared by Erin Karper

Publisher: *Lyn Uhl*
Acquisitions Editor: *Star MacKenzie Burruto*
Assistant Editor: *Cheryl Forman*
Managing Technology Project Manager:
Stephanie Gregoire

Managing Marketing Manager: *Mandee Eckersley*
Senior Content Project Manager:
Samantha Ross
Production Service: *Nesbitt Graphics, Inc.*
Printer: *West*

ISBN 1-4130-1179-9

Thomson Higher Education
25 Thomson Place
Boston, MA 02210-1202
USA

For more information about our products,
contact us at:
**Thomson Learning Academic Resource
Center 1-800-423-0563**

For permission to use material from this
text or product, submit a request online at
http://www.thomsonrights.com

Any additional questions about permis-
sions can be submitted by email to
thomsonrights@thomson.com

Contents

Technology Toolboxes   xi
Preface   xiii

Part 1   Understanding the Basics

CHAPTER 1   Nouns and Articles   1

Nouns   1
Articles   2
Nouns and Articles Synthesis   3

Level One Exercises
1.1 Common Nouns in Simple Sentences   5
1.2 Count and Noncount Nouns in Simple Sentences   7
1.3 Collective Nouns in Simple Sentences   9
1.4 Abstract Nouns in Simple Sentences   11
1.5 Articles and Determiners in Simple Sentences   13

Level Two Exercises
1.6 Nouns, Articles, Determiners   15
1.7 Unclear Noun and Article Errors   17

CHAPTER 2   Pronouns   19

Types of Pronouns   19
Pronoun/Antecedent Agreement   21
Vague Pronoun Usage   22
Differentiating Who/Whoever and Whom/Whomever   22

Level One Exercises
2.1 Personal, Indefinite, and Reflexive Pronouns   25
2.2 Interrogative, Demonstrative, and Reciprocal Pronouns   27
2.3 Pronoun Cases   29
2.4 Turning Vague Pronouns into Specific Elements   31
2.5 Who/Whoever, Whom/Whomever   33
2.6 Pronoun Case and Agreement   35

Level Two Exercises
2.7 Pronouns and Antecedents   37
2.8 Pronouns and Antecedents   39

CHAPTER 3   Verbs and Verbals   41

Verb Types   41

Verb Tense   43
Verbals   44
Subject-Verb Agreement   45
Mood   48

Level One Exercises
3.1 Verb Tenses and Main and Subordinate Clauses   51
3.2 Auxiliary Verbs and Linking Verbs   53
3.3 Choosing Correct Verb Tenses   55
3.4 Regular Verb Tenses   57
3.5 Participles and Participial Phrases   59
3.6 Infinitives and Gerunds   61
3.7 Subject-Verb Agreement: Simple and Compound Subjects, Tenses, Infinite and Collective Nouns   63
3.8 Subject-Verb Agreement: Linking Verbs, Measurements, Subjects Ending in –s, Antecedents, Relative Clauses   65
3.9 Passive and Active Voice   67

Level Two Exercises
3.10 Verb and Verbal Forms   69

CHAPTER **4**   **Modifiers**   71
Adjectives   71
Descriptive Adjectives   71
Adverbs   72
Dangling Modifiers   74

Level One Exercises
4.1 Adjectives   75
4.2 Adverbs   77
4.3 Dangling Modifiers   79

Level Two Exercises
4.4 Revising Modifiers   81

CHAPTER **5**   **Commas**   83
Marking Independent Clauses   83
Commas in Introductory Clauses   84
Commas Between Items in a Series: Coordinate Elements and Coordinate Adjectives   84
Commas Between Coordinate Adjectives   85
Commas with Nonrestrictive Elenments   86
Commas with Parenthetical and Transitional Phrases   86
Commas with Contrasts, Interjections, Direct Address, and Tag Sentences   87
Commas in Quotations, Names, Titles, and Correspondence   87
Misused Commas   88

Level One Exercises
5.1 Commas in Independent and Main Clauses   91
5.2 Independent Clauses and Coordinating Conjunctions   93

5.3 Commas in Introductory Clauses and in a Series   95

5.4 Commas between Coordinate Adjectives and to Set Off
Nonrestrictive Elements   97

5.5 Commas with Nonrestrictive Elements, Parenthetical and
Transitional Phrases   99

5.6 Commas   101

Level Two Exercises

5.7 Commas   103

CHAPTER **6**   **Other Punctuation Marks   105**

Colons   105
Semicolons   106
End Punctuation   106
Apostrophes: Possession, Contractions, Plurals   107
Quotation Marks for Quoting, Dialogue, Titles   108
Dashes, Parentheses, Ellipses   109

Level One Exercises

6.1 Colons   111
6.2 Semicolons   113
6.3 End Punctuation: Period, Question, Exclamation   115
6.4 Apostrophes   117
6.5 Quotations Marks, Dashes, Parentheses, Ellipses   119

Level Two Exercises

6.6 Punctuation Review   121

Part 2   Putting the Pieces Together: Writing Sentences
and Paragraphs

CHAPTER **7**   **Constructing Basic Sentences   123**

The Sentence   123
Correcting Sentence Fragment Writing Habits   124
The Clause   125

Level One Exercises

7.1 Simple Sentences   127
7.2 Simple Sentences   129
7.3 Appositive and Prepositional Phrase Fragments   131
7.4 Dependent and Independent Clauses   133

Level Two Exercises

7.5 Dependent and Independent Clauses   135
7.6 Revising Sentence Fragments   137

CHAPTER **8**   **Fragments, Run-on Sentences, Comma Splices,
and Fused Sentences   139**

Sentence Fragments   139
Run-on Sentences   140

Level One Exercises

8.1 Identifying Fragments   143
8.2 Revising Sentence Fragments   145
8.3 Revising Sentence Fragments   147
8.4 Correcting Dependent Clause Fragments   149
8.5 Repairing Comma Splices and Fused Sentences   151
8.6 Identifying Comma Splices and Fused Sentences   153
8.7 Identifying Run-On Sentences   155

Level Two Exercises

8.8 Fragments, Comma Splices, and Fused Sentences   157

CHAPTER 9   **Simple to Complex Sentence Patterns**   159

Coordination   159
Subordination   160
Transitional Words or Phrases   161
Correlative Conjunctions   162
Semicolons and Colons   162

Level One Exercises

9.1 Building Complex Sentences with Coordination   165
9.2 Building Complex Sentences with Subordination   167
9.3 Building Complex Sentences with Transitions   169
9.4 Building Complex Sentences with Semicolons and Colons   171
9.5 Building Complex Sentences   173

Level Two Exercises

9.6 Building Complex Sentences   175

CHAPTER 10   **Parallelism**   177

Parallel Items in a Series   178
Parallel Items in Pairs   178
Parallelism in Lists and Outlines   178
Parallelism in Headings   179
Revising Faulty Parallelism   179

Level One Exercises

10.1 Parallelism in Items within a Series   181
10.2 Revising Faulty Parallelism   183
10.3 Parallelism in Pairs, Lists, and Headings   185

Level Two Exercises

10.4 Revising Faulty Parallelism   187

CHAPTER 11   **Writing Clearly, Cleanly, and Concisely**   189

Wordiness   189
Unnecessary Use of Self   190
Clichés   190
Unnecessary Repetition   190

Level One Exercises

11.1 Eliminating Wordy Prose   193

11.2 Eliminating Clichés   195

11.3 Eliminating Clichés and Personal References   197

11.4 Eliminate Wordiness and Repetition   199

Level Two Exercises

11.5 Eliminate Wordiness and Repetition   201

CHAPTER **12**   **Word Choices to Enhance Your Writing**   203

Public Discourse   203

Private Discourse   204

Colloquialisms   204

Slang   204

Regionalisms   205

Simple and Safe to Elegant and Sophisticated Vocabularies   205

Level One Exercises

12.1 Public Discourse: Formal/Informal Writing   207

12.2 Slang, Colloquialisms, and Regional Dialect   209

12.3 Enhancing Your Vocabulary with Verb Choice   211

12.4 Enhancing Your Vocabulary   213

Level Two Exercises

12.5 Enhancing Your Vocabulary   215

CHAPTER **13**   **Writing Solid Paragraphs**   217

Paragraph FAQs   217

Transitions: Create Paragraphs Using Time, Spatial, or Logical Order   220

Level One Exercises

13.1 Identifying Paragraph Elements   225

13.2 Creating Topic Sentences   227

13.3 Ordering Paragraphs   229

13.4 Signal Transitions   231

Level Two Exercises

13.5 Writing Solid Paragraphs   233

Part 3   **The Bigger Picture: Essays and Other Writing Projects**

CHAPTER **14**   **Writing within Established Contexts**   235

Defined Purposes and Specified Audiences   235

Create Tone to Match Your Audience and Purpose   237

Using Evidence to Support Your Claims   238

The Academic Genres   239

Level One Exercises

14.1 Matching Appropriate Audiences to Purposes and Tones   241

14.2 Blending Evidence with Your Work   243

14.3 Choosing Genres to Audiences, Purposes, and Tones   245

Level Two Exercises
14.4 Matching Appropriate Genres to Audiences, Purposes, and Tones 247

CHAPTER **15** **Writing Thesis Statements** 249

From Statement to Thesis Statement 250
Let the Thesis Create a Map of Your Paper 251
Let Your Outline Guide Your Thesis 252
Thesis Sentence Style Options 252
Matching Discipline and Genre to Thesis Statement Styles 253
Thesis Checklist 253

Level One Exercises
15.1 Create a Thesis from Topic and Paper Ideas 255
15.2 Crafting Thesis Statements 257
15.3 Create a Thesis from an Opinion 259

Level Two Exercises
15.4 Expanding Vague Thesis Statements 261

CHAPTER **16** **The Parts of the Essay** 263

The Preamble 263
The Beginning: The Introductory Paragraph 264
The Middle or the Body 266
Conclusion Techniques 271

Level One Exercises
16.1 Introductory Paragraphs 273
16.2 Introductory Paragraphs 275
16.3 Arranging Paragraphs for Clarity 277

Level Two Exercises
16.4 Concluding Paragraph Exercises 279

CHAPTER **17** **Writing the Research Essay** 281

You, the Dominant Voice 281
Blending Outside Research with Your Voice 282
Varying the Blending Language 284
Summarizing 284
How to Punctuate a Quotation 286
Parenthetical and In-Text Source Citations 287

Level One Exercises
17.1 Blending Quotations and Dominant Voice 289
17.2 Varying the Blending Language 291
17.3 Appropriate Summarizing 293
17.4 Paraphrasing 295
17.5 Integrating Sources into Sentences 297
17.6 Practicing with Voice 299

Level Two Exercises
17.7 Creating a Research Package 301

CHAPTER 18 **Revision Strategies** 303

The Language Revision Process 304
Editing Grammar and Mechanics 307

Level One Exercises
18.1 Revising for Audience 309
18.2 Revising for Word Choice and Variety 311
18.3 Revising for Clarity 313
18.4 Revising for Tone 315

Level Two Exercise
18.5 Revision Exercises 317

Part 4   **Make Your Rhetoric Electric**

CHAPTER 19 **Writing with Technology** 319

Maximizing Papers with Fonts, Lists, and Emphases 319
Electrifying Your Text with Visuals 322
Inserting Pictures, Graphs, and Other Visual Enhancements 323
Desktop Publishing 325

Level One Exercises
19.1 Analyzing Fonts 327
19.2 Making Lists 329
19.3 Headings and Emphases 331
19.4 Visual Designs 333

Level Two Exercises
19.5 Desktop Publishing: Creating a Brochure 335

CHAPTER 20 **Visual and Oral Presentations** 337

The Importance of Memory 337
Speaking Strategies 338
Creating Visual Rhetoric 339

Level One Exercises
20.1 Revising the Written into the Spoken 341
20.2 Making Your Presentation Memorable 343
20.3 Making Visual Aids 345
20.4 Determining the Rhetorical Situation 347

Level Two Exercises
20.5 Turning the Print into Visual/Oral Presentations 349

CHAPTER 21 **Rhetoric on the Web** 351

Using Email Effectively 351
Creating Identity on the Internet: Listservs, Blogs, Wikis, *Facebook,
    MySpace, YouTube, Xanga*, and the List Goes On 354
Writing and Designing Web Pages and Sites 356

Level One Exercises

21.1 Effective Email Techniques 359

21.2 Effective Email Text 361

21.3 Effective Discussions and Blogs 363

21.4 Making Web Appropriate Content 365

Level Two Exercises

21.5 Analyzing Blogs 367

Technology Toolboxes

Customizing Your Word Processing Desktop   2

Working with Multiple Windows   20

Speller and Grammar Check   49

Organizing Your Files   74

Displaying File Information   89

Inserting Page Numbers, Headers, and Footers   110

Checking for Sentence Fragments   126

Highlight Potential Errors   141

Checking for Sentence Errors   163

Inserting Headings into Your Writing   179

Find and Replace   191

The Spelling and Grammar Advanced Functions   205

Keyboard Composing Advantages   219

Keeping Track of Online Research URLs   238

Tracking Your Revisions   254

Using the Comment Feature   272

Organize Your Research Leads   282

Peer Revision with Track Changes and Comments   307

Embedding Screenshots   323

Creating Diagrams, Charts, and Graphs   325

Making a Brochure   326

Bullets and Lists   339

Email Etiquette   351

Preface

As you begin using *The Thomson Handbook Workbook*, think about how you have been filling up your academic day planner with due dates for writing assignments from various classes. Each one probably needs you to adjust to a new scenario, set of instructions, form, and context, and you must decide how to best approach each task. As a teacher, a writer, and a former student, I recognize how real-world authors constantly have to react to different writing situations. I wrote *The Thomson Handbook Workbook* to assist you in navigating through all of your college courses and your life outside and after college by helping you strengthen the writing skills you already possess. Part of this goal includes demonstrating how you can use technological tools to enhance your writing process and the finished product in whatever shape it may take, from an essay you write for class, to a visual presentation for work, to a personal blog you create to share your thoughts and opinions with the world.

The brief introductory information and exercise sets in *The Thomson Handbook Workbook* were designed to help you build upon your knowledge of the fundamentals while advancing your skill level so that you can tackle the new and more sophisticated demands of college writing. As already experienced authors, you know that before you begin and throughout the time you manage your various writing projects, you must understand how nouns, verbs, articles, adjectives, and the other grammatical and mechanical elements function together to help you create simple and complex sentences, paragraphs, and papers. These speech parts form the foundational elements authors must engage in order to create simple and complicated pieces of writing, from a quick email to a professor to a ten-page argument paper with a Web text visual component. In essence, often the difference between a sharply crafted, well-received piece of writing and one that fosters confusion and misunderstanding are mistakes in grammar and style that obscure creativity and ideas.

Organization

- **PART ONE Understanding the Basics**

  Because good writers are well versed in the fundamentals, Part One allows writers at all levels to advance by reviewing basic skills associated with the parts of speech and grammar, concepts we have been exposed to throughout our careers as students.

Topic	Thomson Handbook Workbook	Thomson Handbook
Nouns and Objects	Chapter 1	Chapters 40, 60
Pronouns and Antecedents	Chapter 2	Chapter 43
Verbs	Chapter 3	Chapters 45, 61
Modifiers	Chapter 4	Chapter 46
Commas	Chapter 5	Chapter 48
Other Punctuation Marks	Chapter 6	Chapters 49–53

- **PART TWO Putting the Pieces Together: Writing Sentences and Paragraphs**

Part Two asks you to flex your composition muscles and to apply the fundamentals to the sentence and paragraph levels. Beginning with Chapter 7's "Constructing Basic Sentences," you will apply your knowledge of the parts of speech to create clear, clean, and concise sentences.

Topic	Thomson Handbook Workbook	Thomson Handbook
Constructing Basic Sentences	Chapter 7	Chapters 33, 36
Fragments, Run-on Sentences, Comma Splices, and Fused Sentences	Chapter 8	Chapter 40
Simple to Complex Sentence Patterns	Chapter 9	Chapters 36, 37
Parallelism	Chapter 10	Chapter 34
Writing Clearly, Cleanly, and Concisely	Chapter 11	Chapter 36
Word Choices to Enhance Your Writing	Chapter 12	Chapter 38
Writing Solid Paragraphs	Chapter 13	Chapter 5

- **PART THREE The Bigger Picture: Essays and Other Writing Projects**

Once you establish your confidence in crafting strong sentences and paragraphs, you are ready to put all your knowledge into moving your work into bigger venues like essays and research papers for all your classes.

Topic	Thomson Handbook Workbook	Thomson Handbook
Writing within Established Contexts	Chapter 14	Chapters 1, 7, 9–13
Writing Thesis Statements	Chapter 15	Chapter 4, 14
The Parts of the Essay	Chapter 16	Chapters 2, 4
Writing the Research Essay	Chapter 17	Chapters 14–23
Revision Strategies	Chapter 18	Chapter 6

- **PART FOUR Make Your Rhetoric Electric**

The finest writing cannot be appreciated unless its authors make their work available for others to read. Today's writers must manage word processing programs, oral and visual programs, and the World Wide Web to move their ideas from thoughts to papers, presentations, and Web pages. Part Four guides you through the variations between the print discourse you have been perfecting and the digital discourse you can employ to enhance your work.

Topic	Thomson Handbook Workbook	Thomson Handbook
Writing with Technology	Chapter 19	Chapters 24, 25
Visual and Oral Presentations	Chapter 20	Chapter 26
Rhetoric on the Web	Chapter 21	Chapters 27–32

Features

- **Technology Toolboxes**

Throughout the workbook you will find **Technology Toolboxes,** tips that help you utilize all the technological tools your computer, word processor, and the Internet have to offer. Because style and visual presentation enhance writing, the toolboxes offer sound advice to customize your screen and options, change your font choice, embed images into a paper, create your own graphs, and employ many other features.

- **Tiered Exercises**

  The workbook provides two tiers of exercises, a **Level One** set per chapter that helps you recognize, practice, and gain control of the information presented in the chapter, and the more difficult **Level Two** exercises which provide a cumulative review of the chapter or invite you to apply your knowledge in more sophisticated venues and—your own writing projects.

- **Partnering with the rhetorical handbook for composing in the digital age**

  The Thomson Handbook Workbook cross references *The Thomson Handbook* for an integrated approach to writing instruction designed to provide extra opportunities for review and practice. Each chapter of *The Thomson Handbook Workbook* refers to material covered in greater depth in *The Thomson Handbook*, and often examples found in the handbook are summarized or condensed in the workbook for quick and easy review. *The Thomson Handbook Workbook, The Thomson Handbook,* you, and your professor are a cohesive team dedicated to helping you write as clearly, cogently, skillfully, and effectively as possible. I am honored to be part of such a noble endeavor with you. Happy writing!

Acknowledgments

Everything I do, including this book, is dedicated to "the twins," my biggest fans and the two people most responsible for the person I am today: my wonderful mother, June Ross Walters Wright, whose gentle and loving guidance began me, and my aunt, Jean Ross Walters Johnson, who joyfully finished what her sister could not.

Also, I thank my wonderful father, Eugene Walker Wright, for supporting me in all my endeavors, from high school sports to the Ph.D., as well as J. B. Johnson, Robert T. and Janie H. Walters, and Lawrence M. Walters, and the rest of my family for putting up with me all these years.

Aside from my family, many thanks to other kin: Janet Puzz, Tracey Schwarze, Jay Paul, and Joanne Paul for your unflagging support from beginning to end, and Suzy Phillips and Debbie East who enthusiastically celebrate all my projects.

I am most grateful that my students Kristin Brickley, Mike Hilleary, Boone Brosseau, Melanie Beahm, Julie Johnson, and Danielle Brigida bravely allowed me to use their papers as examples.

Much appreciation goes to Leslie Taggart, Development Editor of *The Thomson Handbook,* for generously consulting on the project early on. Special gratitude to Cheryl Forman for her keen editorial instincts and excellent advice as she directed the development of this workbook, and thanks to Kathy Smith for her sharp editing skills.

Finally, I am indebted to my colleagues, Rebecca Wheeler and Jessica Clark, for working the exercises.

Nouns and Articles

The Thomson Handbook, **Chapters 40, 60**

All writers must understand how nouns and articles affect the writing process in order to create subjects that agree with verbs and nouns that agree with antecedents (what they refer to).

Understanding how nouns react with other words in your sentences helps you write without errors, no matter the context.

Nouns

Common Nouns

- Individuals or groups of people: the **students,** the **crowd,** a **woman**
- Places: the **neighborhood,** the **campus,** the **library**
- Things: a **pep rally,** a **party,** the **meeting**

Proper Nouns

Specific person, place, or thing and always capitalized

- **Rosa Parks**
- **Birmingham, Alabama**
- **Freedom Ride**

Count (Countable) Nouns

Nouns that can be counted

- three **books**
- one **opportunity**
- 25 **people**
- 7 **days**

Noncount (Uncountable) Nouns

Nonquantifiable nouns typically in singular form

- **space**
- **time**
- **snow**

- **information**
- **homework**

Collective Nouns

Typically singular units that define a group: **faculty, family, cabinet, board**

Abstract Nouns

- Define an intangible concept: **love, equality, friendship, peace**

Articles

- Act as a signal to indicate a noun follows
- Definite article: "the" **the** tabby cat
- Indefinite article: "a, an" **a** tabby cat

An article, any one of the pronouns, a possessive noun, or a number is called a *determiner* when it explains, identifies, limits, or qualifies general and specific nouns.

- **The** class took **an** exam. (article)
- **Her** scores disappointed the professor. (personal pronoun)
- **Margarita's** class did well on the exam. (possessive noun)
- **This** course is more difficult than the one I took last quarter. (demonstrative pronoun)
- **Which** guidelines apply to the paper? (interrogative pronoun)
- **Both** John and Roark spoke at the conference. (indefinite pronoun)
- **Which** book did you finish first? (relative pronoun)
- Jennie was ranked **first** in her class (number)

Technology Toolbox

Customizing Your Word Processing Desktop

Before you begin writing your papers, take a few minutes to customize your word processor's screen. Begin by familiarizing yourself with all the buttons and drop-down menus at the top of the screen. You will find that you use some more than others. For example, the drop-down choice, "File," which contains options to open new and existing documents, save, print, and change the page format, is necessary, whereas "Table," which allows you to create a table to hold data, might be less important depending on the tasks you want to accomplish.

The buttons above the drop-down menus enable you to perform quick activities without searching. The tiny diskette icon prompts you to save your file, the small printer shoots you to the printing options, the scissors are for cutting text, and the clipboard lets you paste text. Most word processors can be set up with at least four top rows of buttons and menus, three at the bottom, rulers at the left and top margins, and a palette at the right to display recently written documents and additional options.

Nouns and Articles Synthesis

Person: President **John Fitzgerald Kennedy** delivered a famous speech in 1963.

Place: He spoke to citizens in **Berlin, Germany.**

Thing: Kennedy wanted his **topic** to inspire Berliners.

Count Noun: That **single** afternoon in Berlin did wonders for relations between the countries.

Noncount Noun: When Kennedy uttered "Ich bin ein Berliner," which translates to mean "I am a citizen of Berlin," the **crowd** erupted into cheers.

Abstract Noun: The **speech** indicated that Americans stood in **support** of their German allies.

Article: In **the** middle of the Cold War, Kennedy spoke about **a** topic important to the world.

Determiner: Both President and Mrs. Kennedy spoke to the crowd that day.

For more information about President Kennedy's trip to Berlin, Germany in 1963, go to 1c "Context Shapes the Writer's Purpose" in *The Thomson Handbook.*

Level 1

Name_____ **Date**_____

DIRECTIONS Underline all the common nouns in the following sentences. Some sentences may contain more than one common noun.

SAMPLE

Scott and Kara bought their <u>puppy</u> a <u>ball</u>.

1. Kate needed a part-time job, so she applied at Schooner's.

2. The manager hired her on the spot and gave her a uniform and instructions.

3. She quickly discovered waiting tables is difficult.

4. People are often demanding and the hours are long.

5. Many customers do not realize servers make less than minimum wage and count on their tips.

6. Customers who tip less than 15% send a signal to the server that she did not perform a good job.

7. Many servers believe they get blamed for problems in the kitchen, such as cold food, wrong orders, or other issues.

8. In the restaurant business, servers getting behind in their work is called being "in the weeds."

9. Servers have to report their income to get credit with the government.

10. Kate and her friends like their jobs because they get paid in cash.

11. They also get free sandwiches and salads when they work.

Level 1

Name_____ **Date**_____

DIRECTIONS Underline all count nouns twice and noncount nouns once in the following sentences.

SAMPLE

President Franklin Roosevelt explained in his first inaugural <u>speech,</u> "The only thing we have to fear is <u>fear</u> itself."

1. Roosevelt is the thirty-second President.

2. At age 39, Franklin became ill with polio.

3. He exhibited courage and determination to overcome the crippling disease.

4. Roosevelt's era will forever be marked by political and personal turmoil.

5. Roosevelt's two dogs, Major and Fala, lived in the White House.

6. Roosevelt was the first president to appoint a female cabinet member.

7. His fifth cousin was Theodore Roosevelt, and he was a fourth cousin once removed to Ulysses S. Grant.

8. His four sons served in World War II.

9. Roosevelt's first and second New Deal programs pulled the nation out of the Great Depression.

10. Roosevelt's wife, Eleanor, became a tremendous political leader too, presiding over many policies for human rights in numerous nations outside the United States.

Level 1

Name_____ **Date**_____

DIRECTIONS Underline all collective nouns once in the following sentences. Some sentences may contain more than one example or none at all.

SAMPLE

The <u>committee</u> voted to pass the amendment.

1. The residents of Sharon's hall think of themselves as family.

2. Some are from the freshman class and others are sophomores.

3. Regardless of their ages, the girls are a crew.

4. Like family, some are loners and others stick to the group for assurance and help.

5. Yesterday the president held an assembly and invited faculty to present their views.

6. The campus ROTC's five units and 50 members participated in the halftime parade.

7. The wind ensemble performed a solo.

8. Cheerleaders encouraged the crowd to perform the wave.

9. One section of Amber's hall painted their faces in school colors.

10. The Homecoming Parade can only move as fast as the lead team.

11. Homecoming Weekend gives parents an opportunity to see school spirit in action.

12. The weekend events include a pep rally to introduce the football team and crown the Homecoming King and Queen, the football game, a formal dance, and a picnic.

Level 1

Name_____ Date_____

DIRECTIONS Underline all abstract nouns once in the following sentences. Some sentences may contain more than one example or none at all.

SAMPLE

   Oscar Wilde once quipped, "<u>Life</u> imitates <u>art</u> far more than <u>art</u> imitates <u>life</u>."

1. Kara commented that fear guides many people.

2. Television news programs promote anger and helplessness.

3. Talking about prejudice makes some people uncomfortable and uncertain in their views.

4. Often trust is the key to a healthy conversation and open dialogue.

5. Students admired Tracey's bravery for speaking out against campus racism and homo-phobia.

6. Hopefully, curiosity will encourage more to join the conversation.

7. Some believe passion and hope will combat anger and fear.

8. Arguments of truth and justice continue to plague the quest for equality.

9. Rebecca saw a bumper sticker that read "Freedom is not free" and wrote the message on the board for a discussion on democracy.

10. Another student added a quote by Mahatma Gandhi, who once said, "My life is my mes-sage" to further the discussion.

Level 1

Name_____ **Date**_____

DIRECTIONS Underline all articles and determiners once in the following sentences. Above each, define which form is used. Some sentences may contain more than one example.

SAMPLE

Indef.   *Art.*
Jay and Joanne <u>each</u> contribute to <u>the</u> gardening chores.

1. Jay's jobs include cutting the grass and weeding.

2. Making sure the birds are fed is Joanne's favorite task.

3. Both do some of the planting, but each has specific strategies on the best methods.

4. Sunflowers are their favorite flower, and there are six varieties in their flowerbed.

5. Many gardeners share whatever plants they have in abundance, so some of Jay and Joanne's specimens are now in Mary's garden.

6. Mary's Aunt Jean loved Queen Anne's Lace, which is a member of the wild carrot family.

7. Mary transplanted two Queen Anne's Lace plants into her yard and now there are fourteen new plants.

8. The Black Swallowtail butterfly lays her eggs on Queen Anne's Lace.

9. The eggs, which begin no larger than a speck of pepper, grow into larvae, which eat the leaves from Queen Anne's Lace and from parsley, too.

10. Then the plant becomes both home and food source for the growing caterpillars.

Level 2

Name_____ **Date**_____

DIRECTIONS The following paper contains various examples of nouns and articles and contains errors. Underline all nouns and circle all articles and determiners.

Last summer Jean and Marsha decided to go on a road trip. Each knew which fantasy destination she wanted, but decided to research individually and present findings together. What neither knew was that they were in complete agreement the whole time!

Marsha first used her sister's laptop to research beach destinations with golf courses, then narrowing her search to Virginia Beach, Virginia and Nags Head, North Carolina. She wanted as much information as possible to find the vacation destination that included fun and relaxation.

Independent from Marsha, Jean chose three popular vacation spots: Virginia Beach, Nags Head, and Hilton Head, South Carolina. Jean's research included boating and hotel information, in addition to golfing excursions and available beaches.

Together the girls laughed when they saw their goals were so similar and ended up going to Virginia Beach for a week of fun and adventure. While in the resort city they took a whale watching cruise on the *Miss Virginia Beach*, which was an opportunity of a lifetime because they saw several of the most beautiful whales playing in the ocean. Fortunately, Marsha had a waterproof camera and captured some amazing shots.

Level 2

Name_____ **Date**_____

DIRECTIONS The following paragraphs contain various errors regarding nouns and articles, some of which make the paper unclear and hard to understand. Identify and replace the problem words with the correct terms.

Barak Obama, the Junior Senator from Illinois, is one of the few in the senate to use the Web as a way of communicating with his constituents and people who want to learn more about him.

The son of divorced Parents, Obama stayed with his mother in Hawaii and lost contact with his father who moved to his Native Kenya. Obama moved to mainland America to begin gaining his college knowledges, eventually becoming the first African American Editor of the Harvard Law Review. He also is only the third African American elected to the senate since reconstruction.

Obama's policy favor working-classes, and he has dedicated his career to improving person's Civil Rights, Personal Rights, and Working Families. A example of his policy is found in a issue about prisoner's rights. After he found out some of Death row inmates were actually not guilty, Obama got legislations passed requiring all capital murder interviews must be Videotaped.

Thanks to his Web Site, everyone can read Obama's blog and find his truths. He is currently working on the environmental issues and planet's welfare by helping to create plan for energy independence. On his blog he compares America addiction to oil like alcoholism. We can't admit we are the alcoholics and then skip the 12-Step Program, so Obama proposes we get business in on the conversations.

Biofuels need to come out of the labs and if the business fund the labs, we can get alternative fuel option sooner. The next plan he sees important is cleaner burning coal, so Obama has the solutions to help solve the energy crisis.

In addition to his Blog, a option to listen to him speak can be found by following the Podcast Link on the senate web site. By using web Barak Obama has found the way to reach his audiences almost immediately.

Interrogative Pronouns

This pronoun class asks a question.

> **Who, what, which, whom, whose, whoever, whatever, whichever**
>
> **What** is your favorite football team?
>
> To **whom** do we owe this honor?

Demonstrative Pronouns

These words refer to a particular item or group of things.

> **This, that, those, these**
>
> **This** salad is delicious because the ingredients are fresh.
>
> Some of **those** dinner specials are outrageously expensive.

Reciprocal Pronouns

These pronouns identify a relationship between two or more individuals.

> **Each other, one another**
>
> My parents deeply respect **one another.**
>
> The team learned how to rely upon **each other** during difficult games.

Pronoun/Antecedent Agreement

Pronouns must agree with their antecedents, so a single pronoun (**I, myself, you, me, she, her, he, him, it, oneself**) must refer to a single antecedent (**Dave Matthews, the drummer, the lead singer, a fan**).

Plural pronouns (**them, they, their, us, we**) must refer to plural antecedents (**The Dave Matthews Band, fans, people**).

Compound Antecedents

Typically, compound antecedents, which are two or more antecedents, are plural and therefore require a plural pronoun.

> **The Dave Matthews Band and Robert Randolph and the Family Band** kick off **their** summer tour June 3.

In some cases the compound antecedent is a single person, thing, or idea and requires a singular pronoun.

> Dave Matthews, **singer and farmer,** lives on **his** farm in Charlottesville, Virginia.

When connecting single antecedents with *each, every, or, nor,* or *neither,* use a single pronoun.

> Like The Grateful Dead and Phish, the band's Warehouse Fan Association allows **its** fans to purchase concert tickets in advance.

If the collective noun antecedent is singular, use a singular pronoun.

> The **band** published **its** tour dates early this year. *(The band is considered a single unit in this instance.)*

The concert **audience** ran to claim **their** spots at the front of the hall. *(The audience may be a group but here they are acting as individuals.)*

Vague Pronoun Usage

Most writers rely on pronouns like *it* and *they* to refer to antecedents. Such practices help authors vary their sentences and reduce repetition, but problems occur when writers over-use and depend so much upon these pronouns that the reader no longer knows what the antecedent references.

In writing that uses pronouns clearly, it is immediately obvious to what a pronoun is referring:

Janet loves the Impressionist painters because **they** painted in a dreamy and romantic style.

In this case, the plural pronoun *they* clearly refers to the painters because *Janet* is singular.

There are at least ten Monet pieces in museum's permanent collection. **It** may not display **them** all at once, but there are at least five out at any time.

Again, because of plural and singular antecedents, the reader can quickly see that *it* refers to the single antecedent, *the museum,* and *them* refers to the plural antecedent, the *ten Monet pieces.*

In the following sentences it is unclear to which antecedent the pronoun is referring:

There is no way to know which paintings in the collection will be on display, and the docents have very little information about **it.**

It can refer to two separate antecedents, *the collection* or the *display,* and a third one that is implied, which is the process by which the paintings are selected for the display, so this unclear reference causes the reader to stop relying on the author for meaning.

Clarified: There is no way to know which of the collection will be on display, and the docents have very little information about **how the paintings are chosen.**

Now the reader understands that the author means the process used by museum officials to choose which pieces are displayed and when.

This is a very unsatisfactory way to inform the public about the museum's holdings and displays.

In this case, the author's *This* insufficiently stands in for what should be an important point the author wants the reader to understand.

Clarified: **Museum docents are most connected with the public** and must be well informed about the museum's holdings and displays.

This sentence leaves no doubt about the author's intentions.

Differentiating Who/Whoever and Whom/Whomever

To decide which pronoun is most appropriate in your writing, you must know which one is the subject of the clause (*who* or *whoever*) and which is the object (*whom* or *whomever*).

As a quick test to determine which is the correct pronoun to use, substitute in the sentence this equation:

Who = *he* or *she*

Whom = *him* or *her*

If the substitution makes sense, you have chosen the right pronoun.

Who left car windows down?

He left the car windows down.   NOT   **Him** left the car windows down.

The university's chapter of Habitat for Humanity builds homes for **whoever** demonstrates the greatest need. (**whoever** *is the subject of the clause*)

The project foreman consults a structural engineer **whom** he worked with on another Habitat project. *(the foreman is the subject and the* **whom** *is the object).*

Level 1

Name_____ **Date**_____

DIRECTIONS Underline all personal, indefinite, and reflexive pronouns in the following sentences. Some sentences may contain more than one example or none at all.

SAMPLE

> <u>Anyone</u> can see how happy <u>he</u> makes <u>her</u>.

1. Yesterday, the softball team invited everyone from the English Department for a fun match.

2. Jessica volunteered herself and her friends to help coach the faculty members.

3. Her bubbly attitude keeps her teammates laughing through their drills.

4. Many of the faculty played softball at their colleges and almost everyone agreed to the game.

5. After a few practices, Dr. Nichols declared his team ready for whatever was to come their way.

6. Everyone seemed to have a good time, especially students who came to cheer for their favorite professors.

7. The department themselves were surprised at their skills on the field.

8. In the eighth inning with two on base, Roberta hit a triple, making her the hero of the day.

9. One student yelled, "Not bad for a bunch of oldies!" and everyone laughed.

10. Though the English Department gave the softball team a run, it was impossible to beat the girls who had age and training on their side.

Level 1

Name_____ **Date**_____

DIRECTIONS The following sentences contain a variety of interrogative, demonstrative, and reciprocal pronouns. Underline the appropriate pronoun and identify its correct category in the space provided.

SAMPLE

Int.   Dem.
<u>Which</u> of <u>these</u> words best describes your personality?

1. Golf is one of those misunderstood sports.

2. People who do not play golf wonder what golfers see in hitting a little white ball.

3. "Keep your head down, arms straight, and shoulder lined up with the target" are just a few of those things to remember.

4. When asked why he plays golf, Peter shrugged and said, "What's not to like?"

5. Golfers maintain a code of ethics with one another that includes behavior, honor, and whatever other sports conduct rules that apply.

6. Whenever possible, Jean treats herself to new golf balls.

7. Jennifer always wants to know what tee times are available just before lunch.

8. To chip onto the green, which club is better, the 8 iron or a wedge?

9. To those just learning the game, Tracey recommends taking a few lessons.

10. Some people like to challenge the golf course, and others prefer to compete against each other.

Level 1

Name_____ **Date**_____

DIRECTIONS Determine the correct form in each of the following sentences. Underline the correct choice.

SAMPLE

After our laptop was stolen, my parents told my twin sister and [I / <u>me</u>] they would buy the next computer for [<u>us</u> / ourselves].

1. At first our parents blamed my sister and [me / I] for the theft until the university police [who / whom] investigated the crime told them it was not our fault.

2. The news was difficult because [they / their] firstborn children had been burglarized.

3. My father put [himself / hisself] through college, so he knows how tight money gets.

4. Our mother instructed [we / us] to go online and do the necessary research [ourselves / ourself].

5. Computers make researching easy for [we / us] students, but Mom forgot to [whom / who] she was talking to because our computer was stolen!

6. My sister and [me / I] went to one of the computer labs on campus to conduct our research.

7. Though we thought all labs were open to everyone, we discovered some are for specific majors [who / whom] need special software.

8. By restricting labs for certain students, [they / their] are reducing the number of available computers.

Level 1

Name _____ **Date** _____

DIRECTIONS The following sentences contain vague or murky pronoun references. After determining what you believe is the author's meaning, rewrite each sentence for clarity by replacing all vague pronouns.

SAMPLE

Problem

People go to a movie for a variety of reasons. <u>They</u> use <u>it</u> to escape reality, to be entertained, and to learn.

Revision:

People attend movies for a variety of reasons, such as to escape reality,

to be entertained, and to learn.

    Film companies put a lot of money into advertising because it is what attracts fans. Therefore, they should have a channel on television that only shows movie trailers because it would keep them informed about new movies. They are the two- or three-minute versions of movies that explain the plot and make it easier for fans to pick.

    When deciding which movies to watch, it is hard to choose one that will appeal to everyone. For example, some people like slasher flicks because they have a particular kind of humor. On the other hand, some comedies are not funny at all, so that makes it hard when the group wants a funny movie. Because going to the movies costs a lot of money, this means making the wrong choice is expensive, so having the movie channel would make it easier to find the right movie for the right crowd.

_____

_____

_____

_____

_____

_____

_____

_____

_____

_____

_____

Level 1

Name_____ **Date**_____

DIRECTIONS Underline the correct case or word for the pronouns in brackets.

SAMPLE

   In 1925 Virginia Woolf, [<u>who</u> / whom] was a prolific British author, published her novel, *Mrs. Dalloway.*

1. The novel describes the title character [who / whom] is giving a big dinner party.

2. Woolf wrote about the character, [who / whom] lives for a full twenty-four hours in the novel.

3. Mrs. Dalloway is a character modeled after a friend of Woolf's, [who / whom] Woolf thought to be shallow.

4. In 1999 Michael Cunningham, [who / whom] is an American writer, published *The Hours.*

5. [Who / Whoever / Whomever] reads *The Hours* will see the parallels between the two novels.

6. Three characters [who / whom] compete for attention in *The Hours* are connected.

7. [Who / Whom / Whoever] reads *Mrs. Dalloway* should read *The Hours.*

8. Clarissa Dalloway is the character [who / whom] Woolf concentrates, and Cunningham's main character is Clarissa Vaughn.

9. *Mrs. Dalloway* centers on the main character [who / whom] hosts a large dinner party for many of her friends and neighbors with [who / whom] she shares her life.

Level 1

Name_____ **Date**_____

DIRECTIONS The following sentences contain a variety of pronoun errors. Underline the appropriate pronoun form based upon the evidence provided by the sentence and its antecedents.

SAMPLE

> *The Thomson Handbook* features student Gina Wolf and her friend [who / whom] were best friends in elementary school.

1. According to Wolf, the girls ran an after-school "restaurant" of clientele [whom / who] were dolls.

2. After school and on weekends the girls taught [theirselves / themselves] how to stretch [their / her] imaginations through play.

3. As readers, you and [I / me] may not know Gina and Jamie, but we share similar experiences that help [you / us] make meaning from the paper.

4. Most everyone has experienced losing a friend [who / whom] represents something larger than [your / our] lives.

5. Ironically, each of the girls [herself / themselves] learned something about how and why their friendship could not survive their childhood.

6. At the end of the paper [we / I] learn how Jamie, to [who / whom] the paper is written, surprised Gina by remarking about the fort.

7. As readers [you / we] are as touched as Gina because we have only had Gina's perspective to define their personalities.

8. Each of [you / us], the readers and Gina and Jamie [herself/themselves], gains valuable knowledge about how we can carry with us forever our early childhood friendships.

9. Wolf used [their / her] childhood stories to process a broken friendship through research.

10. Even though Wolf knew her professor and classmates would read the paper, [who / whom] did the story serve the most?

Level 2

Name_____ Date_____

DIRECTIONS The following student draft contains errors in pronoun and antecedent agreement, vague or ambiguous pronoun use, and general misuse problems. Find and correct the errors in the space provided.

Jet skis are motorcycles on water, and the people who drive them love the thrill of the speed. Originally called "personal watercraft," Clayton Jacobson, a motocross enthusiast, invented them in the early 1970s. These water rockets became popular to those whom enjoy an individual sized boat for less than a regular boat costs. This explains why there are so many jet skis on the water today.

There are many benefits for you to own one of these. For one, they are much cheaper than a boat, and very light so even one person can launch it by themself. These little boats don't drink a lot of gas, and they are fast enough to pull a skier or even a couple of people on a raft. Also, towing little kids is fun because the look on their face says they are having fun.

It has also been said that jet skiers are menaces on the water, people that dart in between larger boats and they cause accidents. Boaters also expect the other person to be able to read their mind which has nothing to do with types of watercraft and their owners. Finally, the problem that no one seems to want to address is that it is impossible to generalize about which style of boats attracts those whom are more dangerous than others.

Finally, the jet ski enthusiast and the larger boat owner don't share the same water space. For example, my friend Jay and me stay close to shore so we can jump waves, where the guys in the big motorboats and sailboats stay in deeper water where it is safer for them.

Level 2

Name_____ **Date**_____

DIRECTIONS The following student draft contains errors in pronoun and antecedent agreement, vague or ambiguous pronoun use, and general misuse problems. Find and correct the errors in the space provided.

Last summer I worked harder than I ever thought possible. It all started when my cousin showed me a flyer and said me and him could make lots of money in a very short time. If anyone in our family knows how to make quick money, it is him, so I agreed and we reported for work that Monday.

We were assigned to a crew that was painting a water tower out in the country. I don't know who's decision it was to paint a water tower, but that turned out to be one hard job and not at all what I thought Peter and me would be doing. On the first day we were separated into teams. Me and this guy, Scott, was in charge of keeping the paint pans filled for the painters, and Peter and this guy, Jay, were in charge of stocking supplies for them.

Though we thought we were going into nice people's houses to paint and get out of the hot weather, it is good that we didn't since I and Peter did not have any painters experience. Instead, we stayed on the ground that summer and the foreman told us later that either Peter and him or us were allowed to paint the water tower because it was too dangerous for inexperienced kids. Even though we all stayed hot, it was a good time.

Verbs and Verbals

The Thomson Handbook,
Chapters 45, 61, 62

Think of verbs as the energy source of a sentence because without a verb, you have no action and therefore no sentence. Even the most basic sentence must have a verb to express an action or a state of being.

I **waited**.   (state of being)
They **ran.**   (physical activity)
He **grieved.**   (emotional activity)

The same sentences elaborated with more detail:

I **waited** for the show to start.   (state of being)
They **ran** in the Relay for Life marathon.   (physical activity)
He **grieved** for the loss of his dog.   (emotional activity)

Verbs are more complex than nouns and pronouns, which we studied in Chapters 1 and 2. We'll examine some of the reasons below.

Verb Types

Verbs fall into two main categories: **main verbs** and **auxiliary verbs.**

Main Verbs

As their name suggests, the main verb controls the central action in the sentence.

The panther **stalked** her prey.

The verb *stalked* describes a specific method of hunting, and good writers experiment with the best verbs possible to convey meaning. Following are other ways to extend the same or a similar idea.

The panther **hunted** her prey.

The panther **followed** her prey.

The panther **watched** her prey.

Auxiliary Verbs

Auxiliary verbs are also called **helping verbs** because they assist main verbs in making **verb phrases,** which are combinations of verbs and other words. Like all verbs, they can be categorized by tense, voice, or mood. Some auxiliary or helping verb phrases create a

passive voice, a condition where the action of the verb is performed on the subject as opposed to **active voice,** where the subject of the sentence performs the action.

AUX. VB.
If we keep going, we **might find** an open gas station.   (active voice)

AUX. VB.
However, we **should stop** for the night anyway.   (active voice)
The decision to stop **was made** by Janet.   (passive voice)

When an auxiliary verb expresses possibility, probability, ability, necessity, willingness, or obligation, it is a **modal auxiliary.**

Modal Auxiliary Verbs				
be	have	must	shall	would
can	may	need	should	
could	might	ought	will	

We **should drive** as far as possible tonight.   (*signals the subject's willingness*)
I **might need** a nap later.   (*signals the subject's need or necessity*)

Linking Verbs

Linking verbs are so called because they *link* the subject to the subject complement, which is a word or phrase that describes, refers to, or renames the sentence's subject.

The most common linking verb is the *to be* verb:

am, is, are, was, were, has been, are being, might have been

S   LV   SC
Doug **is** looking forward to his vacation.

(Doug *is the subject; is is the verb linking him to his condition of anticipating the vacation.*)

S   S   LV   SC
Robin and Steve **were** happy with their purchases.

(Robin and Steve *is the subject; were links them to their condition of happiness.*)

S   LV   SC
The air **feels** humid today.

(Air *is the subject and the verb links the subject complement by describing how the air feels to the author.*)

S   LV   SC
Sharon **seems** to feel better now.

(*The linking verb describes how Sharon feels: better.*)

Simple Forms of Common Linking Verbs			
appear	believe	prove	sound
are	feel	remain	taste
be	grow	seem	turn
become	look	smell	

Remember, some **linking verbs** are also **auxiliary** or **helping** verbs.

The theater **is located** downtown.   (linking: shows location of subject)

Melanie **is willing** to walk to the theater.   (auxiliary: indicates ability and willingness)

Verb Tense

There are two issues involving verbs that plague writers: verb tenses, which we will discuss now, and subject-verb agreement, which we cover later in this chapter. Regardless of whether the verb is regular or irregular, the following are the tenses that verbs can take.

———3 MAIN TENSES———			——————— 3 SECONDARY TENSES ———————		
Present	**Past**	**Future**	**Present Perfect**	**Past Perfect**	**Future Perfect**
run	ran	will run	has/have run	had run	will have run
eat	ate	will eat	has/have eaten	had eaten	will have eaten
fly	flew	will fly	has/have flown	had flown	will have flown

Tenses in sentences look like this:

Present	I **volunteer** for Relay for Life.
Past	Imogene **volunteered** for Relay for Life.
Present Perfect	Linda **has volunteered** for Relay for Life.
Past Perfect	Jim **had volunteered** for Relay for Life.
Future Perfect	Jennifer **will have volunteered** for Relay for Life.

Most verbs are *regular,* which means they follow a predictable tense pattern like the example above where the endings (also called *inflections*) are the same. This means past and all three perfect tense verbs end in *–ed*, and progressive and present participles, which we will study later this chapter, end in *–ing*.

Irregular verbs are not predictable, which baffles non-native speakers learning English as well as native speakers.

Common Irregular Verbs					
awake	drive	make	run	take	withhold
become	fall	meant	say	think	withstand
begin	forgive	overdo	send	undergo	wring
bite	freeze	overhear	shake	underwrite	write
break	grow	partake	shine	unwind	
buy	hide	proofread	sleep	wake	
catch	hurt	prove	spill	weep	
cut	keep	read	spring	win	
deal	lay	repay	strike	wind	
draw	light	ride	sweep	withdraw	

Present	Enrique **rides** his bike to school when weather permits.
Past	Margarita **rode** to school with Sharon.
Present Perfect	Peter **has ridden** the subway most of his life.
Past Perfect	John **had ridden** from Pittsburgh to Philadelphia recently.
Future Perfect	By the time she is 21, Jennifer **will have ridden** the same bus for 15 years.

Verbals

Present and Past Participles

A *participle*, which can be either present or past tense, is a verb acting in a sentence as an adjective or a noun.

Present tense participles end in *–ing,* and past participles end in *–ed, –en, –d, –t,* or *–n.* For example, used as a verb in the present tense, *love* means having a deep affection.

Cheryl **loves** her new kittens, Xavier and Nora.

Add *–ing* to make a present participle, and the word changes meaning slightly.

Xavier and Nora have been adopted into a **loving** home.

Now the verb functions as an adjective to describe a place of deep affection instead of the affection itself.

Add *–ed* and the past participle of *love* still serves as an adjective in this use.

Xavier and Nora are much **loved** kittens.

Adopting them seems like a long **awaited** journey.

More Present Participle Examples

Studies show that pets provide their owners with a **calming** influence. *(Calming describes the influence.)*

Rules for Participial Phrases

1. When participles become **participial phrases,** things become a bit more complicated. The rule of thumb is to keep the participial phrase as close to the noun it modifies as possible.

   Unclear:
   Having been a pet owner all her life who understands the value of pets in the home is Cheryl. (Cheryl *is too far away from the phrase describing her.*)

   Clear:
   Having been a pet owner all her life, Cheryl understands the value of pets in the home. (Having been a pet owner *is a participial phrase describing* Cheryl.)

   Unclear:
   Sleeping under the bed was Nora and Xavier noticed and joined her.

   Clear:
   Xavier noticed Nora **sleeping under the bed** and joined her. (Sleeping under the bed *modifies* Nora.)

2. The participial phrase should consist of the participle, modifiers, complements, and objects.

PRES. PART.	PREP.	ART.	IND. OBJ.
Sleeping	**under**	**the**	**bed**

3. Set off or surround a participial phrase with commas when it: (a) starts a sentence, (b) occurs in a sentence as a nonessential element, or (c) is located at the end of a sentence and is separated from the word it modifies.

Having been a pet owner all her life, Cheryl understands the value of pets in the home. (set off with a comma)

Xavier, **trying to become the king of the household,** tries to dominate Nora especially around the food bowl. *(The participial phrase is not essential to understanding the sentence or its meaning.)*

Cheryl often observes Nora and Xavier interacting, **though she understands staying out of their drama is best for all.** (she *refers to Cheryl, not Nora*)

Infinitives

Also in the category of verbals are infinitives, "to" plus the verb, which functions as an **adjective, adverb,** or **noun.** Verbals can also serve as the sentence's **subject, direct object,** or **subject complement.** Identifying the infinitive should not be hard since the pattern is typically *to + verb* (unless you separate the two parts and create a split infinitive), but determining its function in the sentence requires deeper analysis.

As with all verbs and verbals, misunderstanding infinitives will undoubtedly create errors in your writing.

The director asked the cast **to rise** when the lead actor began his soliloquy. (**adjective** to modify the noun *cast*)

Jamie has four papers **to write** before final exams. (**adjective** modifying *papers*)

Joseph made the flight because he gave himself enough time **to drive.** (**adjective** modifying *time*)

Janet took a nap **to restore** her energy. (**adverb** modifying *took*)

We must speak up **to be** heard. (**adverb** modifying *speak*)

To stop the car at that point seemed dangerous. (**subject**)

Suzy and Debbie wanted **to fly** to Las Vegas, but flights were too expensive. (**direct object**)

Jean's goal is **to beat** her best race time by five seconds. (**subject complement**)

Gerunds

Gerunds are verbs that always end in *–ing* and always function as nouns.

Lou recently learned the art of **soldering.**

Public **speaking** terrifies many.

Steve Prefontaine was one of the most influential athletes in the sport of **running.**

Roberta finds **cooking** to be a way to relax after a long day at school.

Subject-Verb Agreement

The **subject** of a sentence must agree in number with the **verb** in the sentence. However, subject-verb agreement is one of the biggest problems plaguing college writers today.

To create grammatically solid sentences, a singular subject must have a singular verb form and a plural subject must have a plural verb form. In other words, nouns and verbs used in the same sentence must match to be considered correct.

Examples:

	SUB. VB.
Single Subject-Verb Agreement	Rick takes guitar lessons regularly.
	SUB. VB.
	Lynne cooks a homemade meal every night.
	SUB. VB.
	A tomato plant thrives better with regular care.
	SUB. VB.
Plural Subject-Verb Agreement	Rick and Missy take guitar lessons from the same teacher.
	SUB. VB.
	Lynne and her mother cook a homemade meal every night.
	SUB. VB.
	Tomato plants thrive with regular care.

Decisions about which verb goes with which subject get more complicated because of **verb tenses, irregular verbs, linking verbs, compound subjects** (more than one subject in a sentence), and different sentence formats where subjects and verbs are not so easily identifiable.

As previously discussed in the section "Verb Tenses," as well as in *The Thomson Handbook*, Chapter 45, verbs have several tenses.

Present	The bald eagle **is** no longer endangered.
Past	The bald eagle **was** endangered for many years.
Present Perfect	The bald eagle **has been making** a comeback in recent years.
Past Perfect	The bald eagle **had been** victim of pesticide use.
Future Perfect	The bald eagle **will have made** a remarkable comeback if its numbers continue to rise.

Note that in each of the preceding examples, *the bald eagle* is a single subject taking a singular verb.

Now notice the differences in the sentences when using a plural subject.

Present	Bald eagles **are** no longer endangered.
Past	Bald eagles **were** endangered for many years.
Present Perfect	Bald eagles **have been making** a comeback in recent years.
Past Perfect	Bald eagles **had been** victims of pesticide use.
Future Perfect	Bald eagles **will have made** a remarkable comeback if its numbers continue to rise.

Compound subjects can be either singular or plural, depending on the conjunctions used.

Plural Compound Subjects

Scientists and environmentalists joined forces to save bald eagles from extinction.

Neither scientists nor environmentalists expected the surviving eagles to bounce back so quickly.

Singular Compound Subjects

Each scientist and each environmentalist working on the bald eagle project **is** now pleased.

Not every scientist or environmentalist believes the fight to save the birds is over.

The Environmental Protection Agency as well as the Sierra Club has its own story about how the eagles were saved.

To further complicate matters, some authors create sentences so that the verb comes before the Subject.

VB.   SUB.   VB.   SUB.

Over the mountain top glides the eagle. —OR— Over the mountain top glide the eagles.

Indefinite pronouns and **collective nouns** can complicate matters even more because writers must not only understand the context, but also make sure that context is apparent to their readers. Basically, most indefinite pronouns are singular and require singular verbs, but there are exceptions to this rule.

Anybody who lives in the building **is** eligible for a free parking space.

Each must **take** responsibility for his or her actions. *(plural)*

Each takes responsibility for his or her actions. *(singular)*

Half of the audience **is** rooting for Florida State, and the **other half are** for Ohio State.

The **faculty are** supportive of the student government initiatives.

The **faculty supports** student government initiatives.

Authors make mistakes **when subjects and their verbs are separated** by other clauses and phrases. Make sure you reread your work, scanning especially for the subject to agree with its verb.

Incorrect:

SUB.   VB.

The **birds,** after scouting a nesting site and building their new home, often **begins** trying to make a family.

Correct:

SUB.   VB.

The **birds,** after scouting a nesting site and building their new home, often **begin** trying to make a family.

Subject and Linking Verb Agreement

When a linking verb appears in the sentence, the same rules apply because the linking verb also denotes singular or plural status.

That injured female bald **eagle is making** a quick recovery at the wildlife rescue center.

A **family** of eagles, after scouting for months, **has built** a nest in some loblolly pines at the Botanical Gardens.

Subjects Using Measurements and Verb Agreement

Context determines whether the measurement or numerical subject is plural or singular.

One half of the play **is** devoted to a historical recreation of the colonists landing at Jamestown, Virginia. *(The subject is half of a single play.)*

Three years have passed since I saw Daryl. *(plural because the number of years is more than one)*

Singular Subjects Ending in –s: As writers and readers, we intuitively see words ending in –s as plural, but that rule is not always the case with many nouns.

The **United States is** involved in a dangerous war with Iraq.

Economics is helpful to understanding business and the stock market.

Agreement with Titles, Names, and Words Used as Words: Each of these is considered singular and takes a singular verb.

Operation Smile helps children born with cleft palates and other facial defects.

Yorktown, Virginia is a city with much colonial and Revolutionary War history.

Agreement in Relative Clauses: Some clauses that contain the relative pronouns **who, whom, whose, which,** or **that** require the same verb as their antecedent (the word for which the pronoun stands).

      ANT.   VB.

The **person** who most **deserves** the award for leadership is Kristin.

      ANT.   VB.

The **six people** who almost lost their lives in the avalanche **are** doing better now.

Mood

Writers use tone to create mood, but sentence structure and verb forms also create mood.

Indicative mood expresses an opinion or a fact, asks a question, and is the most frequently used of the three moods.

Reality television has practically destroyed the popularity of the sit-com. *(opinion)*

Jorge shut the door in the salesman's face. *(fact)*

Where are his manners? *(question)*

Imperative mood is used for giving orders and directing requests.

Stop at the store on your way home.

Use a napkin please.

Stop!

Subjunctive mood is practically obsolete in writing and speech today and appears only in certain circumstances when the author is expressing a wish or refuting a statement. Subjunctive verbs are **present tense,** where the verb stays in the present regardless of its subject, or **past tense,** which also remains in the past tense regardless of the subject.

Yesterday, Elena's mother strongly suggested that she **clean** her room before asking any favors. *(present subjunctive even though the sentence is reporting a past event)*

I wish I **were** graduating this year. *(past subjunctive because first person past tense should be* was*)*

Active and Passive Voice

Voice is determined by whether the subject of the sentence performs an act (*active*), or the subject receives the act (*passive*).

Active Voice
Manuel ate the cake.
Lizzie kissed her sister good night.
Polio killed many people.

Passive Voice
The cake was eaten by Manuel.
Her sister was kissed good night by Lizzie.
Many people were killed by polio.

Because active voice is stronger and more direct than passive voice, always try to convert your sentences to active construction so the emphasis remains on the subject performing the action.

However, in some cases passive voice is preferred, such as when the subject is less important than the rest of the information in the sentence, or the subject is unknown.

Cancer was found in the blood culture. *(emphasis on the cancer and not who found it)*

This incredibly important novel was written by an unknown author. *(The novel, not the fact that the author is unknown is the feature.)*

Technology Toolbox

Spelling and Grammar Check

Mastering verbs and verbals takes persistence and practice, and is also a process you and your computer can work on together.

Your word processor's "Tools" menu contains a Spelling and Grammar checker that you can either turn on all the time or use when you need to. If you decide to activate the device, you will find red and green squiggly lines under misspelled words, grammatically incorrect sentences, and even spacing problems. While you are writing a draft, ignore the errors because you need to concentrate on content. After you have written a draft and are satisfied with your work, activate the checker.

Warning! No software program is foolproof, so make sure you consult *The Thomson Handbook* to resolve grammatical problems before you submit your papers for evaluation.

Level 1

Name_____ **Date**_____

DIRECTIONS The following sentences contain a variety of verbs. Underline each action verb and identify its correct tense below the word. Some sentences contain more than one verb.

SAMPLE

Present   *Present*   *Present*

<u>Choosing</u> names for family pets <u>requires</u> lots of thinking and <u>reflects</u> the family's personality.

A majority of families own at least one family pet, usually a dog or a cat. For some, finding the right match is difficult, while others fall in love with a certain furry face at first sight. Depending on the owner's personality and needs, some prefer to buy an animal from the local pound while others order from breeders. Some want a show dog or cat and others want a family friend. Small children, elderly occupants, and other considerations affect what kind of animal the owners select. Just like the long process of discovering the right pet for the family, naming that pet requires a good deal of thought too.

Our culture enjoys a long relationship with its animals, and from that we see how matching the right pet to the right family and the right name for the right pet means a great deal. In thinking about the best name, people subscribe to several strategies. First, there are the typical pet names. Back in the old days *Fido* was a big dog name, but today many cats respond to *Mr. Whiskers* or *Miss Kitty*, and lots of dogs come when called *Happy* or *Buster*.

When stumped for a name, it is natural to look to the pet's physical attributes or its personality for clues. White-footed dogs and cats might be named *Socks*, as in former President Bill Clinton's cat, or *Boots*. All white cats and dogs might be called *Snowball*, or *Whitey*, and all black ones *Blackie* or *Oynx*. Dalmatians and spaniels answer to *Spot* or *Freckles*. Tabby cats appear to have eyeliner that extends from under their eyes, so a popular name for them has been *Cleopatra* or *Cleo* for short. People who own 3-legged dogs sometimes dub them *Tripod* or *Trip*. A boisterous animal might be identified as *Reckless*, or *King*.

Others believe certain more traditional people names speak to their pets' personalities. These people might own a *Sam*, a *Butch*, or a *Sally*. Without knowing, the famous and the literary lend their names, like *Elvis, J-Lo, Elton,* or *Sinatra, Olivier,* and *Hemingway*. People label so-called tough dogs *Capone, Scarface,* or *Hobo*, and other pets live up to regal names like *Lady, Queenie,* and *Simba*.

Finally, there is a small but original group of people who subscribe to true people names for their animals. These folks feed and house *David, Marsha,* and *Jessica*. They eschew the strategies other pet owners adopt, preferring to mix things up a bit in the naming process by not following tradition.

Level 1

Name_____ **Date**_____

DIRECTIONS The following sentences contain a variety of auxiliary and linking verbs. Underline each type of verb. Some sentences contain more than one kind.

SAMPLE

linking
Vegetarianism <u>is popular</u> in many Western cultures.

1. Hundreds of millions of people are trying vegetarian diets.

2. Vegetarians can adopt as little or as much of the eating lifestyle as they want.

3. There are no strict guidelines despite what some strict vegetarians might say.

4. A diet high in vegetables, fruits, and nuts is quite healthy for people of all ages.

5. Kristin thought that once a person becomes a vegetarian, she should remain one forever.

6. Though quite popular since ancient times, vegetarianism seems stigmatized.

7. Mary will help you find good sources of information if you are interested.

8. Numerous Web sites devoted to vegetarian recipes are easy to find, and the main cooking networks are good sources too.

9. Almost every cultural cuisine is vegetarian friendly, so finding restaurants that offer options should be easy.

10. For people who might be worried about protein, tofu, beans, and nuts are excellent sources and can be added to most dishes.

Level 1

Name_____ Date_____

DIRECTIONS The following paragraphs contain choices for verb tenses in regular verbs. Underline the correct choice for each sentence. Use the context found in the sentence for clues.

SAMPLE

In spring 2006 a group (will go / <u>went</u>) to Belgium and France.

1. Each year students (take advantage / took advantage) of the study abroad program.

2. Kristin and Mike (were / will be) part of that last trip.

3. They (discover / discovered) how different their lives (will have been / were) in comparison to the Belgian students they met.

4. The experience (is / will have been) one they will never (forgot / forget).

5. Kristin (choose / chose / chooses) lots of gifts for her family and friends.

6. She (find / finds / found) coasters, scarves, and chocolate at a small shop near the hotel.

7. She (buys / buy / bought) a wonderful print of the Eiffel Tower when she and Mike (takes / took / will take) a side trip to Paris, France.

8. Then she (make / made / makes) sure not to wrinkle the print while sightseeing.

9. While in the Louvre they (listens / listened) to the guide (explains / explained / explain) stories about the paintings.

Level 1

Name_____ **Date**_____

DIRECTIONS In the following sentences underline the incorrect verb in the parentheses.

SAMPLE

Peter (<u>use</u>, used) to live in California.

1. Now he and his family (live / lived / lives) in Virginia.

2. Being close to the water (reminded / remind / reminds) them of where they used to live.

3. Peter (is / am) an avid windsurfer, so he (go / goes / went) to the beach often.

4. He (finds / found) a group of windsurfers to hang out with and (makes / made) new friends.

5. The guys (explains / explained) how water currents near the fishing pier (is / are) dangerous to windsurfers and surfers.

6. Under the pier there (is / are) concrete jetties that (catch / caught) the sand.

7. These jetties (is / are) dangerous because they can (broke, break) a surfer's board easily.

8. However, many people (surf / surfs / surfed) near the pier because the jetties (creates / create / created) good waves.

9. Peter (figured / figure / figures) people (took / take / takes) that risk for better wave action, but he (decide / decided / decides) to (go / went / goes) elsewhere.

10. Sometimes Peter's family (go / goes / went) along for the day.

11. When the water (is / are) calm, Peter and Christine (puts / put) their sons on the board to (teaches / taught / teach) them windsurfing.

Level 1

Name_____ **Date**_____

DIRECTIONS Underline the participle or participial phrases in each sentence and draw a line to indicate the noun or pronoun that is being modified.

SAMPLE

<u>Trying to get a better deal</u>, Tracey searched online for her books.

1. After final exams many students left for home but others decided to go to a theme park featuring some of the biggest roller coasters ever.

2. June, Jean, J.B., and Bunk packed themselves into one crowded vehicle, and Bobby, Janie, Dick, and Helen loaded up the other car for the anticipated journey.

3. Once in the park, the group investigated the variety of rides before committing themselves to the long lines.

4. Jean and June found themselves staring at the top of the ride, told the others they would sit this one out.

5. Gathering up speed, the roller coaster began its initial descent.

6. Looking over the car she was in, Janie realized she wished she was on the ground with the twins.

7. Mesmerized by the thrill of the coaster's power, Bobby did not realize Janie was clutching his arm in terror.

8. Jean and June, determined to ignore the group's teasing, led the charge to the second biggest coaster in the park.

Level 1

Name_____ Date_____

DIRECTIONS The following sentences contain a variety of infinitives and gerunds. Circle all gerunds and underline all infinitives. Some sentences contain more than one verbal.

SAMPLE

Inf.   *Ger.*
Since she learned how <u>to cook</u> healthy meals, Katie became passionate about her (eating.)

1. Investing in land has become a real passion for Karen.

2. Because she wants to become a serious buyer, she knows she must curtail her spending on anything that takes away from her investing.

3. After taking a class about how to invest in cheap properties, Karen spent many nights conducting online research to help her find real estate.

4. To be such a wealthy person at such a young age has been trying for Karen, because she can't go shopping with her friends like she used to.

5. Finding proper advertising is a challenge because many current property owners do not want to be contacted.

6. In her spare time Karen loves to poke around in antique shops.

7. She loves nothing better than finding antique cameras to add to her collection.

8. Cleaning these vintage cameras can be daunting, but Karen knows how to handle the delicate pieces.

Level 1

Name_____ Date_____

DIRECTIONS Underline the subject in each sentence and circle the correct verb that agrees with the subject from the selections provided.

SAMPLE

Many photographers [make / makes] their living taking pictures of celebrities.

1. This issue and others regarding the treatment of celebrities [is / are] under constant debate.

2. Some believe the media [have / has] a right to photograph celebrities in public places.

3. However, journalists as well as photographers [has been / have been] known to hide in trees in an effort to get a picture or gossip.

4. Some [claim / claims] that these photographers caused the accident that killed Princess Diana of Great Britain.

5. Celebrities like Angelina Jolie and Brad Pitt [has / have] sued some photographers and won.

6. Catching celebrities doing odd or unusual things [sell / sells] according to some.

7. In the celebrity business, each singer, actor, or actress [is / are] aware of the problems that come with their star status.

8. A celebrity family, after spending a good deal of time and energy avoiding public places, often [move / moves] to a rural setting.

Level 1

Name_____ Date_____

DIRECTIONS Circle the subject in each sentence and underline the correct verb that agrees with the subject from the selections provided.

SAMPLE

(Queen Latifah) has made a CD using her real name, Dana Owens.

1. Latifah, [whom / who] first hit the music scene with a debut album entitled "All Hail the Queen" at age eighteen, quickly became a star in the music and film industries.

2. At the time, she said her main goal with all of her music [was / were] portraying positive images of African American women.

3. Latifah took a lot criticism from the hip-hop industry in order to prove her claim that African American male artists [are / were] degrading females with their music and videos.

4. However, Latifah and her manager [have stood / has stood] by her decisions to use her talents for political purposes.

5. Their decision must be seen as positive because three of her five discs [has / have] gone gold, and she has won a Grammy and been nominated for numerous other awards.

6. She is one of many artists who [has / have] integrity.

7. Her sixteen movies [has / have] established Latifah as an important movie star.

8. Half of the audience at a Queen Latifah concert [is / are] there for hip hop music and the other half [is / are] there for the show tunes.

9. The crowd [is / are] never disappointed when the Queen takes the stage.

Level 1

Name_____ **Date**_____

DIRECTIONS The following sentences have errors concerning either active or passive voice. Correct each sentence in the space provided below it.

SAMPLE

The *Mona Lisa* is considered by art critics one of the finest paintings ever.

Art critics consider the Mona Lisa one of the finest paintings ever.

The famous portrait *Mona Lisa* was painted by Leonardo da Vinci between 1503 and 1505. That time period is called da Vinci's second Florentine period. Much has been written about the painting, the painter, and even the subject. The woman who was the subject of the painting was a young woman from Florence named Mona or Monna Lisa. She was married to Francesco del Giocondo, shortly before she became one of the most well known subjects ever. The portrait was considered the first of the Renaissance portraits, and because of that it has been one of the most copied paintings ever. After being stolen from the Louvre museum in 1911, the painting was found two years later in a hotel in Florence. Since then, efforts to keep the *Mona Lisa* secure and safe have been successful.

_____

_____

_____

_____

_____

_____

Level 2

Name _____ **Date** _____

DIRECTIONS The following sentences have unspecified verb and verbal errors. Correct the errors on the next page in the space provided.

Because they could not stay in their dorm room over the summer, Shanna as well as Jen begin looking for an apartment. Because the girls do not have good employment history, it was noticed by them that landlords can be prejudiced. Shanna, whom's father owns a large swimming pool business, and Jen, whom's father owns a consulting firm, does not think they should have this problem. Two-thirds of the university's students is making an attempt to find a place to live at the same time, so the girls' work has been cut out for them. Finding an apartment has became a competitive process, but the girls and Shanna's father has a plan.

First, a suggestion was brought up that the girls wrote resumes to submit to prospective landlords. This way their qualifications would have been readily accessible and on paper. Then it was suggested that they dress up each and every time one or the other go to view an apartment. That way the landlord, or a person sent in his or her place, see the seriousness of Shanna and Jen to get a good apartment. Finally, the girls understand how finding an apartment is been a hard but worthwhile process.

By trying hard to respond to an industry they know nothing about, Shana and Jen demonstrated they have standed up to the scrutiny. Once they worked on their approach an apartment was available to them for immediate occupancy.

Modifiers

The Thomson Handbook, Chapter 46

At first, adjectives and adverbs seem rather uncomplicated because their central job is to modify, which means they add description, color, depth, and addition to your work. Upon closer inspection, you will see that these simple parts of speech connect with and establish a relationship with almost every word in your sentences by sharpening your meaning through precise and exact wording.

Adjectives

Adjectives modify mostly nouns and pronouns by describing, defining, qualifying, limiting, or enhancing. These words describe how something smells, feels, looks, tastes, and seems. Adjectives basically answer questions like "How many?" "Which one?" "What kind?"

> *Enrique:* "Let's buy one of those beach balls."
>
> *Margarita:* "Which one? There are at least fifteen choices!"
>
> *Enrique:* "Oh, how about the **red** one?"
>
> *Margarita:* "Enrique! I see at least five red beach balls!"
>
> *Enrique:* "Okay, let's buy the **small, red** beach ball with **yellow stripes.**"
>
> *Margarita:* "Now you're talking."

Adjectives can be divided into two classes: descriptive adjectives and determiners.

Descriptive Adjectives

These adjectives identify a specific quality of the noun or the pronoun they modify.

> Even though the play was **lengthy,** we enjoyed ourselves.
>
> John bought **black leather dress** shoes to wear to graduation.
>
> I remember nights sitting on the **cool** sand watching the horizon.

Descriptive adjectives can also be formed from proper nouns.

> The **Federal Period** architecture is prominently featured in homes throughout Salem, Massachusetts.
>
> My mom bought a CD featuring **Gregorian** chants.

Determiners

You will no doubt recognize these adjectives because most of them are **articles, pronouns,** and **numbers.** When they serve as adjectives, they are called *determiners*.

Articles: a, and, the

The sun cast **a** shadow.

Possessive adjectives: add 's to a singular noun and s' to most plural nouns

Jane's accident was serious but not life-threatening.

Possessive pronoun adjectives: my, your, his, her, its, our, their

Her jaw was broken and had to be wired shut.

Demonstrative pronoun adjectives: this, these, that, those

This restaurant serves the best guacamole.

Interrogative pronoun adjectives: what, whose, which

Which recipe did you follow for this dip?

Indefinite pronoun adjectives: another, each, any, both, some, any, many

I can always find **another** job if this one does not work.

Relative pronoun adjectives: which, whichever, whose, whoever, what, whatever

Which book do you think my dad will like better?

Number Adjectives: one, two, three, first, second, third

Do you still remember your **first** kiss?

Adjective Clauses

In more complicated sentence structures, authors use adjective clauses, which are groups of adjectives and adjectives in the **comparative degree** (comparing two things, with the modifier carrying the ending *–er* or using the word *more* or *less*), or **superlative degree** (comparing more than two things, with the modifier carrying the ending *–est*, or using the word *most* or *least*).

Of the two candidates, Pat seemed **more qualified.** *(comparative)*

Of the five candidates, Pat seemed the **most qualified**. *(superlative)*

With all these choices, you can see how easily confused we can get when trying to clarify our meaning to our readers. Problems occur with the order in which the words appear, and the best strategy is to place the adjective after the word it modifies.

Incorrect:
The Bistro has **more better** food than Ralph's Chicken Hut.

Revised:
The Bistro has **better** food than Ralph's Chicken Hut.

Adverbs

Like adjectives, adverbs modify by describing, giving greater detail, or enhancing. The parts of speech the adverb modifies are verbs, adjectives, other adverbs, complete phrases, clauses, and sentences.

Like adjectives, adverbs answer questions like "How?" "Why?" "When?" "How much?" and so on. Many adverbs end in –*ly*, but that is not a hard and fast rule. Basically, locating adverbs in a sentence or learning how to use them effectively requires learning the parts of a sentence.

The quarterback **quickly** threw the ball. *(The adverb describes how the quarterback threw and is located immediately in front of the verb.)*

The backfield moved **expertly** to guard the quarterback. *(The adverb describes how the players moved and is located immediately after the verb.)*

The quarterback's **loudly** called plays could be heard over the crowd. (*The adverb describes how much energy the quarterback expelled and modifies the adjective* called.)

Predictably, we won the football game with no problem. (*The adverb describes in what way the action occurred and modifies the entire sentence.*)

Interrogative Adverbs

These adverbs ask the questions *how, why, when* and *where*.

How did you get that answer?

When did you get in last night?

Where is the movie showing?

Why don't you stay home tonight?

Conjunctive Adverbs

Joining two independent clauses requires a conjunctive adverb. Since the adverb links the two clauses, it can appear anywhere in the sentence at the point where one clause ends and the other begins. You may join sentences with conjunctive adverbs by using a semi-colon or by starting a new sentence. This decision is a matter of style and involves looking at sentence length and form.

The dining services contract was renewed; **therefore** the kitchen and serving staff will not lose their jobs.

The dining services contract was renewed. Therefore the kitchen and serving staff will not lose their jobs.

Representatives for dining services and the university administration were pleased with the outcome; **indeed,** the event turned out positive.

Representatives for dining services and the university administration were pleased with the outcome. **Indeed,** the event turned out positive.

Common Conjunctive Adverbs			
accordingly	furthermore	meanwhile	similarly
also	hence	moreover	still
anyway	however	nevertheless	then
besides	incidentally	next	thereafter
certainly	indeed	nonetheless	therefore
consequently	instead	now	thus
finally	likewise	otherwise	undoubtedly

Dangling Modifiers

When a single adjective or adverb becomes displaced, it has nothing to modify and thus "dangles." This error typically occurs when we try to describe something but then allow other phrases or words to come between our modifier and the word or phrase we intend to modify, or we simply leave out the word or phrase to be modified.

Tip: If your sentence does not have an animate object (a person, animal, etc.), you might be in danger of creating a dangling modifier.

Confusing:

Having seen the movie twice, the ending was still a mystery. *(Here it appears that the ending saw the movie.)*

Clarified:

Having seen the movie twice, I still thought the ending was a mystery. *(Now the sentence is populated with someone or something capable of action.)*

Confusing:

Eating my breakfast, my ride left me.

Clarified:

Eating my breakfast made me miss my ride.

Confusing:

Well ahead of schedule, the plane landed.

Clarified:

The pilots landed the plane well ahead of schedule.

Technology Toolbox

Organizing Your Files

Organize your writing projects so you do not spend needless time searching for that psychology paper whose title you cannot remember! First, create folders (sub-directories that hold files and documents) on your computer desktop or in your My Documents folder. Label each folder by class name, such as "Composition," "History," "Chemistry," and "Theater." When working on a paper, remember that the smart name you thought of at the moment needs to be less clever and more practical as well as unified in using capital letters and spaces. For example, in your "Composition Folder," instead of naming the file "First Argument Paper," which does not explain the content or "How Blogging is Cool," which is wordy, choose a name that accurately describes the paper and can be recognized easily like: "argument_one_blog"

Level 1

Name_____ **Date**_____

DIRECTIONS Underline the adjectives in the following sentences and draw an arrow to the word or phrase these adjectives modify.

SAMPLE

Each year the government warns that we are in store for a long season of terrible colds.

1. In my biology class, several sniffly students complained of sore throats.

2. June, the main complainer, seems to keep a cold longer than anyone else.

3. I wonder, is she unlucky or just unhealthy?

4. I must be healthy as a horse, because I never catch a cold.

5. My mother thinks our Mallicottee genes are the answer to my health because her ancestors were all strong and healthy people.

6. Just in case, I always start the day with a tall drink of orange juice, and I take a daily multivitamin.

7. Doctors suggest frequent hand washing with antibacterial soap is an excellent way to stay healthy.

8. Though I am a sleep-deprived college student, I also try to get eight hours of uninterrupted sleep.

9. You would think my father is a hypochondriac by the care packages he sends me containing Vitamin C drops and store coupons for juice and medicine.

Level 1

Name_____ **Date**_____

DIRECTIONS After reading the following sentences, circle the correct adverb and mark through the incorrect choice. When a sentence contains no choice, circle the adverb and draw an arrow to the word it modifies.

SAMPLE

Caroline runs (~~quick~~, (quickly)).

1. Though featured prominently in the ancient Greek Olympics, running has (slow / slowly) become a major sport.

2. Several magazines devoted to aspects of running feature (comprehensively / comprehensive) written articles.

3. Meb Keflezighi is almost the greatest male long distance runner today.

4. Over 90,000 people actually registered for the 2006 New York Marathon; however, only about one-third will be accepted.

5. I watched Paula Ratcliffe's amazingly fast win in the 2003 London Marathon.

6. Running shoes must be (appropriate / appropriately) designed for the individual's foot strike and gait.

7. Always go to a store specializing in running apparel because the knowledgeable staff can (careful / carefully) monitor your stride and match it to the correct shoe.

8. Wearing cotton socks is a huge no-no because they cause blisters; instead, choose performance socks that efficiently wick away moisture and keep your feet dry and happy.

Level 1

Name_____ **Date**_____

DIRECTIONS The following sentences contain dangling modifiers. Correct each one in the space provided by adding necessary words and/or rearranging order.

SAMPLE

Adjusting the car seat, the pedals are easily reachable.

Adjusting the car seat will enable you to reach the pedals easily.

1. Exhausted from the flight, the trip was finally over.

2. Employed immediately out of college, the job was perfect.

3. After hearing the cat meow, the food bowl was filled up again.

4. Discovered in psychology class, Linda became interested in the early Thai culture.

5. Believing that she has found an interesting topic for her big paper, the choices between African American spirituals and Native American ceremonies is difficult.

6. Using the best and brightest minds in the university, the school newspaper was produced in record time last week.

7. After the difficult year of school work, summer should be a time to kick back and have fun.

8. The library return policy was changed after two years of overdue books.

9. Without wearing a coat, it was difficult to stay warm at the stadium.

10. Having been absent from class too many times, a doctor's note was needed.

Level 2

Name_____ **Date**_____

DIRECTIONS The following passage contains errors in dangling modifiers or lack of adjectives and adverbs. Correct the dangling modifiers and add adjectives and adverbs where needed.

People entering the university for their first year are called _____. Just out of high school, things are _____ different. _____ away from home causes parents and kids to feel _____ and at the same time _____. Once at school, kids face _____ challenges and are often tested _____. Discipline is needed for living away from home. _____ the alarm clock, _____ laundry, _____ when and what to eat are some _____ decisions. _____, students need to make choices _____ to their personalities. Some _____ students can balance fun and studies while some _____ people cannot. In addition to fun, other students participate in _____, sports, and _____ which take time away from studies. These _____ activities help students participate _____ in the university experience. For anyone, college can be _____, _____, and _____. To achieve success kids should _____ monitor their grades, _____ contact their professors if they experience _____, and _____ take responsibility for _____ choices. Life at the _____ level can be _____ _____ if the person makes _____ decisions.

Commas

The Thomson Handbook, Chapter 48

The comma has long mystified writers of all ages and abilities. One reason people have difficulty understanding when to use a comma and when to avoid using one is that this particular grammatical mark is appropriate in many different instances. When writers do not understand each of those correct places in their sentences, they typically make the following rationalizations:

- I'll write short sentences so I don't have to use the comma.
- I'll put a comma in wherever I would pause for breath if I read the sentence aloud.
- I'll stick commas in different places in long sentences and hope for the best.

Since none of these strategies relies on factual information, we advise our readers to learn the various options about the comma. Once you understand how and when to use commas, your writing will greatly improve because you will also understand the parts that make your sentences work correctly.

As *The Thomson Handbook* explains, writers use commas to help make sense of and organize all the information in a sentence. Think of the comma as the writer's way to create a boundary or mark off sections of the sentence. This chapter covers commas used in these circumstances:

- Marking independent clauses
- Indicating introductory elements
- Between items in a series
- Between coordinate adjectives
- Setting off nonrestrictive elements
- With parenthetical and transitional expressions
- With contrasts, interjections, direct address, tag sentences
- In quotations, names, titles, correspondence
- Comma splices
- Misused commas

Marking Independent Clauses

As explained later in Chapter 7, a **clause** is a group of words containing a subject and a predicate that work and relate to each other. An **independent clause** can stand alone as its own sentence and make grammatical sense, but a **dependent clause** cannot stand alone and must be combined with an independent clause.

Calcium builds strong bones. *(a clause as well as an independent clause)*

Calcium builds strong bones. It helps regulate blood pressure. *(two independent clauses)*

Calcium builds strong bones. And fights colon cancer. *(independent and dependent clauses)*

In a paper, even the two independent clause sentences would look choppy, which is why we employ a **comma** and a **coordinating conjunction** to create a better sentence.

When you link two independent clauses together and use a comma, you must use one of the seven **coordinating conjunctions** with the comma in order to make sense. Always place your comma *before* the coordinating conjunction.

The **coordinating conjunctions** are: **for, and, nor, but, or, yet,** and **so.** An easy way to remember these conjunctions is that their first letters form the word **FANBOYS.** Memorize these parts of speech because you will undoubtedly use them a great deal.

Calcium builds strong bones, **and** it helps regulate blood pressure. *(two independent clauses combined with a coordinating conjunction)*

Incorrect:

I used to love ice cream **but** now I am lactose intolerant. *(missing the comma)*

Correct:

INDEP. CLAUSE   CC   INDEP. CLAUSE

I used to love ice cream, **but** now I am lactose intolerant.

Now I drink soy milk, **and** I eat soy ice cream.

Finding soy milk products in restaurants is not difficult, **for** the increase in popularity has created a high demand.

Some people do not understand the trend for soy products, **nor** do they see the health benefits.

Commas in Introductory Clauses

Introductory phrases and clauses "introduce" the material in a sentence or work as transitions from a previous sentence. Most introductory phrases are **dependent clauses** introducing **independent clauses.**

Although Suzy is not allergic to peppers, she cannot tolerate them in her food.

Because Suzy cannot stand peppers, she has a difficult time in Italian restaurants.

For example, many pasta sauces are made with green or yellow peppers.

Still, Suzy loves Italian food and chooses her food carefully.

Commas Between Items in a Series: Coordinate Elements and Coordinate Adjectives

Coordinate elements are words, phrases, or clauses. In a sentence, if you are listing more than two words, phrases, or clauses that are joined by a **coordinating conjunction,** use a comma after each element. Make sure your lists are always similar items (nouns, verbs, gerunds, objects, clauses, or numbered or lettered items).

A series of nouns:
My favorite pizza toppings are **onions, sun-dried tomatoes, spinach,** and **black olives.**

My favorite omelet ingredients are **tomatoes, spinach,** and **cheddar cheese.**

A series of verbs:
Mary taught her cat how to **fetch, chase, and retrieve** paper balls.

When Janet goes home to Biloxi, she **visits** relatives, **drives** around, and **goes** to the beach.

A series of gerunds:
The vacation package includes **skydiving** from a plane, **hiking** through the foothills, and **swimming** in the river basin.

Mark spends his days **practicing** with the football team, **playing** bass in his band, and **studying** to become a veterinarian.

A series of objects:
To furnish their new apartment the roommates bought **plates, glasses, area rugs, a sofa,** and **throw pillows.**

Rose spends her money on **golf, sushi,** and **clothes.**

A series of modifiers:
Cold, wet, and **scared,** the kittens huddled in a corner of the barn for shelter.

Shawn and Kristin's baby is **healthy, alert,** and **cheerful.**

A series of clauses:
The graduation ceremony was particularly touching because **the speaker was an alumnus, the weather cooperated with cool temperatures and lots of sunshine,** and **the crowd of at least 600 was behaved.**

Karen enjoyed her new job screen printing t-shirts **because she got to work with a lot of creative artists who care about their designs, meet many buyers whose stores specialize in a particular theme or style,** and **work for people who care about their employees.**

A series of lettered or numbered items:
The football team's manager must keep track of **(a)** sports drinks, **(b)** first-aid gear, **(c)** equipment, and **(d)** coaching requests.

When vacationing in Aruba, Joseph planned to **(1)** snorkel, **(2)** deep sea fish, **(3)** rent a moped, and **(4)** relax on the beach.

Commas Between Coordinating Adjectives

Like the items in a series above, use a comma to separate **coordinating adjectives** that occur in a series and modify a single word or word group unless joined by a **coordinating conjunction.**

The old man had a **weathered tan** face. (*both* weathered *and* tan *modify* face)

The old man had a **weathered and tan yet kind and patient** face. (*all modify* face *and are linked by the coordinating conjunctions* and *and* yet*)*

A Coordinate Adjectives Test

To make sure you have correctly punctuated your sentences, perform this test:

- Reverse the word order of the modifiers or add *and* between the modifiers. If the meaning of the sentence is not altered, the adjectives are coordinate and need commas.

  The old man had a **tan weathered** face. *(no change to meaning)*

  The old man had a **kind and patient yet weathered and tan** face. *(no change to meaning)*

- If the sentence's meaning has changed when the order is reversed or *and* is inserted, do not use a comma.

  Five Apache helicopters engaged the enemy combatants.

  Apache Five helicopters engaged the enemy combatants. *(the order disrupts the meaning)*

  Five and Apache helicopters engaged the enemy combatants. *(the order disrupts the meaning)*

Commas with Nonrestrictive Elements

Use a comma to set off nonrestricted elements, which are words or phrases that are not essential to the meaning of the sentence. If the sentence makes the same sense without the nonrestrictive wording, those words or phrases are not essential to the sentence. In this case try to remember nonessential = not important = use a comma.

  My favorite television show is *Lost*, **which I watch faithfully every week.** *(Readers do not need to know how and when I watch the show in order to understand it is my favorite.)*

If the nonrestrictive phrase is located in the middle of a sentence, it must be encapsulated by commas because it could be completely cut out of the sentence.

  On the show Jack, **the lead male character,** is constantly burdened with helping the survivors of a plane crash stay safe. *(Jack's status as the lead character is not the important part of this sentence. If edited out, the reader's meaning is intact.)*

  One of the most interesting characters is Kate, **whom the audience discovers through flashbacks is not who we think she is.** *(Though this speaks to why Kate is interesting, this nonrestrictive element is not the main point of the sentence.)*

Commas with Parenthetical and Transitional Phrases

Similar to nonrestrictive elements, parenthetical and transitional phrases are also marked off in the sentence by commas. However, whereas nonrestrictive elements are phrases and clauses, parenthetical and transitional phrases are mostly words and short phrases.

Parenthetical expressions are an author's way of providing a little more explanatory detail to a sentence without going as far as adding a nonrestrictive element.

  Kate, **it is worth noting,** is essentially a good person who has been a victim of a violent past.

  When the plane crashes Kate survives, **as she should,** but the marshal escorting her to jail dies. Viewers could conclude, **naturally,** that Kate is "good" and the marshal is "evil."

Transitional expressions smoothly transport the reader from one point to the next and are very important tools to master.

Incorrect:

Janet found a woman, who will rescue and care for the cat and kittens.

Correct:

Janet found a woman who will rescue and care for the cat and kittens.

- after a subordinating conjunction

Incorrect:

Janet worked hard to find the kittens a home because, she loves animals.

Correct:

Janet worked hard to find the kittens a home because she loves animals.

- with quotations that fit into the structure of the sentence

Incorrect:

Kristin's new motto is, "these are the days."

Correct:

Kristin's new motto is "these are the days."

- with quotation marks that enclose titles

Incorrect:

The quotation comes from the song, "These Are Days" from 10,000 Maniacs.

Correct:

The quotation comes from the song "These Are Days" from 10,000 Maniacs.

Technology Toolbox

Displaying File Information

After a while, the papers and other documents you save will begin to overwhelm you if you do not establish some order in your computer. Even after creating file folders as discussed in Chapter 4's Technology Toolbox, you can easily lose a document. Your word processor's default display shows "tiles" or large images with brief names, but you can reset the default to show your files as "icons," or smaller tiles, by "list" which emphasizes the file name over the icon, by "details" to provide the file size, what kind of file, and the date you last modified. If you still cannot find the paper, go to the folder and under "View" choose "Arrange Icons by" and then "Modified" to put your files in chronological order by date.

Level 1

Name_____ **Date**_____

DIRECTIONS In the following sentences underline any independent or main clauses and insert a comma where needed.

SAMPLE

Jose joined the soccer team for his school and he has become a better player.

<u>Jose joined the soccer team for his school,</u> and he has become a better player.

1. Soccer can be traced back 3000 years to China and it also gained popularity in ancient Japan.

2. The ancient Greeks played soccer but their teams consisted of 27 players each.

3. In the eighth century England modified the game more like the modern version yet Scotland also played a great part in the process.

4. Rumor has it that medieval locals once played soccer with a decapitated human head so one wonders how modern the game was back then.

5. For centuries townspeople played each other violently without fear of punishment so the crowd became increasingly angry on the field.

6. In 1331 King James passed a law against soccer yet even royal proclamation could not stop the fans.

7. But no law could stop the popularity of the sport so the king eventually gave up on the law.

8. In 1815 Eton College established rules and guidelines and these same rules are still in use today.

9. Until 1869 players could handle the ball with their hands so that rule modernized soccer.

Level 1

Name_____ **Date**_____

DIRECTIONS Each numbered sentence set consists of two or more short sentences. Combine the sentences with the appropriate coordinating conjunction and a comma. Rearrange the sentences if you need to.

SAMPLE

Robin believes in superstitions. Robert does not.

*Robin believes in superstitions, so Robert does not.*_____

1. You get bad luck by breaking a mirror. Bad luck comes from stepping under a ladder.

   _____

2. When a dog eats grass it is supposed to rain. Reckless ate grass today.

   _____

3. An itchy nose means company is coming. Some think an itchy nose means you will fight with someone soon.

   _____

4. The luckiest seat in the room faces the door. Lorraine is sitting in the seat facing the door.

   _____

5. Knocking on wood is common superstition. Good spirits living in trees and wood are supposed to help.

   _____

6. Finding a four-leaf clover is good luck. You should look for one.

   _____

7. Walking in the rain brings good luck. It is raining today.

   _____

8. Pick up a penny. You'll have good luck all day long.

   _____

9. In ancient Greek and Roman times ships were christened. This practice is still used today.

   _____

10. Some people are very superstitious. When asked they can't explain why.

    _____

11. Some people think these rituals are silly. Some of them are superstitious too.

    _____

12. What we believe in has a lot to do with how we were raised. Who are we to judge?

    _____

Level 1

Name_____ Date_____

DIRECTIONS Insert a comma where needed in the following sentences. In some cases you must also add a coordinating conjunction.

SAMPLE

Though he knew Joseph was not hurt badly Dave brought his friend bandages and first-aid cream.

Though he knew Joseph was not hurt badly, Dave brought his friend bandages

and first-aid cream.

1. At the ice cream shop Cindy ordered a mint chocolate chip cone Jane ordered a coffee espresso and fudge ripple double dip and Chi-Chi got a dog biscuit.

2. When Salem goes home to see his parents on the weekends he always takes his duffle bag of laundry.

3. At Halloween the hall sponsored a haunted house.

4. Though he is a good skateboarder Joseph has broken his wrist a few fingers and even his collarbone.

5. During one point in the semester Jennie had three midterms and a paper due.

6. In her report on Internet hoaxes Kia's examples included the stolen kidneys the $5 bill at the gas station the Nordstrom cookie recipe and the outdated pancake mix emails.

7. Once Alberto installed spyware software on his computer he noticed the processor speed and the download speed increased dramatically.

8. As the features editor of the school newspaper Amber hired students who had good interview skills and could work under deadline pressure.

Level 1

Name_____ Date_____

DIRECTIONS Insert commas where needed in the following sentences. Then underline all nonrestrictive elements.

SAMPLE

Meteorology the study of weather is a popular major at our university.

Meteorology, <u>the study of weather,</u> is a popular major at our university.

Studying weather patterns has become a wildly popular activity among professionals and amateurs alike. Some say changing environmental conditions such as global warming is causing the Earth's natural atmosphere to change drastically. Most U.S. inhabitants are affected by hurricanes which are increasing in size and strength each year or large unpredictable tornadoes. Other weather phenomena like forest fires and drought affect Midwestern and western states which often suffer years of dry conditions. In order to better understand our conditions meteorologists and scientists insert small data gathering probes into hurricanes and tornadoes. Storm chasers who are either professional scientists or amateur thrill seekers also provide amazingly accurate glimpses into live weather occurrences. Meteorological programs which are quite competitive bring in large funding grants from government agencies and major businesses. Recently a student research team and their professor purchased four brand new boats to further their study of how to protect southern Louisiana from another Hurricane Katrina. Students doing field research find themselves in constant, changing environments. For example teams taking temperature samples from oceans, which help determine whether conditions are right for hurricanes, might put students on a boat in the middle of the Gulf of Mexico at midnight.

Level 1

Name_____ **Date**_____

DIRECTIONS Insert commas where needed in the following sentences. Underline and define whether the sentence contains a nonrestrictive element, parenthetical or transitional phrase in the space provided. Some sentences may contain more than one example.

SAMPLE

Some people think television however is an evil thing.

Some people think television, <u>however</u>, is an evil thing.   <u>Parenth.</u>

1. I believe and this may be counter to popular thought but I don't care that TV provides excellent educational programming.   _____

2. For example on any given day I can learn about how the pyramids in Egypt were built and how tree frogs live in my backyard.   _____

3. However I am also a firm believer that people and who knows what motivates individuals in our culture can become addicted to television to the point that they become unproductive.   _____

4. Moderation to television as in all of life is the key to the problem.   _____

5. Reading naturally is one of the best sources of information but and again we must use our own experience to judge what about all the quality programs about the same educational subjects?   _____

6. Sure there are big problems with television that don't exist with books.   _____

7. Reading for example stimulates the imagination whereas in contrast most agree that television requires no imagination.   _____

8. As someone raised on books and Saturday morning cartoons I admit and you may be surprised to see this I appreciate the memories of reading more than of watching television.   _____

Level 1

Name_____ **Date**_____

DIRECTIONS Correctly punctuate the following passage with commas where appropriate.

Dear Beka

A lot has happened since I saw you last and I just wanted to catch you up on all that has been going on. Basically we are all doing well since moving to Napa Valley California. As you probably know they call this area "wine country" and I can tell you that is the truth. Everywhere we go and there are not many roads because this area is quite rural still we see vineyards. Grape vines of many varieties sizes shapes and styles dot the landscape and during the picking season you have never seen so many people!

Our house is located in Rutherford which is next to Yountville as well as St. Helena. In minutes we can be in downtown Napa which my father calls "a little town with lots of heart" and my mother describes as "the place in which I was born to live" so you can see that my parents are quite happy here. I am too! Of course you've known me all my life which means you know me better than anyone so you know I must be truly happy.

In the fall I start school at Kent State University and I am very excited because I will get to work with Tammy Clewell-Farnan Ph.D. I want to take a critical theory class with her and a British Literature course too.

Well I will close for now.

Love

Daryl

Level 2

Name_____ **Date**_____

DIRECTIONS Correctly punctuate the following passage with commas where appropriate.

After they got paid Tyra Desiree and Alicia decided to host a party and invite some friends over for dinner. The girls pooled their money and took off for the grocery store figuring they would decide the menu when they saw the food. What they did not plan was that each girl had her own pre-conceived idea about what to fix which is to be expected but everyone stayed quiet until they hit the store. "Let's make pasta and salad" suggested Alicia because she loves Italian. When Tyra and Desiree kept walking Alicia tugged on the cart and repeated "I said let's make pasta and salad and you two said nothing."

"Sorry but I was thinking about Thai food because it is healthy easy to make and looks very impressive" responded Desiree.

"Well I thought about buying a little grill and some charcoal and we could fix barbeque chicken corn on the cob and mixed vegetables" said Tyra "and not worry about heating up the kitchen."

Suddenly the girls knew they were in for some discussion though no one figured the problems would start at the store before they could even put the first item in the cart. Because each girl started out firm in her convictions the discussion looked like it would not get very far. However Tyra and Desiree quickly convinced Alicia to abandon her Italian fare which still left the other two menus up for debate.

Eventually the three chose to make Thai food so they would not have to buy a grill and because they already had many of the sauces and spices at home. Since they liked spicy food Alicia picked out three small habanera peppers for the main dish and a bunch of basil to cool things down a bit. After choosing basmati rice tofu red and yellow peppers and broccoli the girls went to the meat counter for some chicken which was the last item on their list.

The dinner party was a great success according to everyone who attended. One of the guests Michael announced "This is the best meal I have ever eaten and I am Food Critic to the Stars Ph.D." and everyone laughed and agreed that the meal was excellent and entertaining. Though they spent too much of their meager pay on such an extravagant feast the three girls were happy and content with their party.

Other Punctuation Marks

The Thomson Handbook, Chapters 49–53

Colons

Use a colon to signal to the reader about new information that lies immediately ahead. Complete sentences that follow a colon are capitalized at the writer's discretion unless the sentence is a quotation that was originally capitalized.

When you introduce a series or a list, a complete sentence or independent clause must come first.

- In a list or series

  I have some distinct memories of the third grade: the cafeteria, kickball, handwriting class, and Mrs. Nottingham. *(The writer clues the reader that she will list those memories.)*

- For explanatory material

  Today in my residential hall meeting I learned an interesting statistic: 75% of the people who live on my hall are from northern Virginia. *(what is more important than the meeting is the fact)*

- To introduce quotations

  In Marilynne Robinson's *Housekeeping,* Ruthie describes the debate about where in the lake a wrecked train came to rest: "Would it sink like a stone despite its speed, or slide like an eel despite its weight?"

- To introduce a second independent clause

  Airport security since September 11 has gone from terrible to much better: recent security installments and more trained dogs and professionals are managing our airports well.

- When **not** to use colons:

  Although *such as, namely, for example,* and *that is* also cue the reader to look ahead, do not use a colon after these expressions.

  Incorrect:
  In the fifth grade I experienced tragedy: for example, both of my grandmothers died as well as my great-aunt.

  Correct:
  In the fifth grade I experienced tragedy: both of my grandmothers died as well as my great-aunt.

In verb and prepositional phrases do not place a colon between the verb and its object or complement or between prepositions and their objects.

  Incorrect:
  After high school Peter traveled to: France, Germany, and the United Kingdom.

Correct:
After high school Peter traveled to France, Germany, and the United Kingdom.

Semicolons

Semicolons express equality or balance between items of equal grammatical importance, such as two independent clauses, two phrases, or lengthy items in a series.

- Between independent clauses

A semicolon is appropriate when the two independent clauses are closely related, are building off of each other, provide similar or opposing information, and are not joined by a coordinating conjunction.

> Diego Rivera painted elements from the pre-Colombian period of Mexican history by using cubism and postmodern art techniques; this juxtaposition in subject and methodology stunned his contemporaries and is still relevant today.

- Between independent clauses using transitional words or phrases

The semicolon is appropriate between independent clauses where the second clause is introduced or uses a word or phrase as a transition.

> Diego Rivera was one of Mexico's most important artists and he married Frieda Kahlo, another one of the country's best artists; **therefore,** people have speculated for years how their creativity inspired each other.

- Separating items in a series

When items in a series use commas or become lengthy enough to confuse readers, use a semicolon.

> Stories about Rivera portray him as a man with a tremendous spirit, as seen in *Marriage of the Artistic Expression of the North and of the South on This Continent; El Vendedor De Alcatraces; The Flower Vendor;* and *Retrato de Ignacio Sanchez.*

End Punctuation

Periods

Although the most common use for the period is to mark the end of a sentence, we also use periods to mark an abbreviation, denote scenes, acts, chapters, verses, or line numbers in dramatic, poetic, and Biblical pieces, and mark Internet url (uniform reference locator) addresses.

- Signal the end of a sentence

  Cotton socks retain foot perspiration.

  I get blisters when I run in cotton socks.

- Indicate an abbreviation

  Bruce S. Gordon is the current president of the N.A.A.C.P.

  At 6 p.m. I am going to the running store on Colley Ave.

- Dramatic, poetic, or Biblical references

  Dramatic: *Rhetorica ad Herennium* IV. Xiv. 20-21.

  Poetic: Lord Byron's "Manfred" Act III. Scene iii. 10

  Biblical: *Jeremiah* 12.1

- Marking electronic addresses

  http://www.google.com

  http://nea.gov

Question Marks

When asking a question or indicating that a date or number may not be accurate, use a question mark at the end of the question.

What time are you leaving?

"Why are you so late getting home?" asked Mom and Dad.

Originally attributed to Cicero, *Rhetorica ad Herennium* is from the second decade of the first century B.C. (?)

Exclamation Points

Exclamations indicate strong emotion or emphatic statement, interjection, or command.

Stop! You can't go any farther on this road.

After Steven and Erin's performance the audience leapt to their feet crying, "Bravo! Spectacular!"

Note: Except to duplicate an emotion witnessed at an event or scene or replicating dialogue, do not use exclamation points in your college writing.

Apostrophes: Possession, Contractions, Plurals

The apostrophe serves in three distinct circumstances:

1. To create or indicate possessive case of nouns and indefinite pronouns

   The **dog's** nose is wet. *(indicates the owner of the wet nose is a dog)*

   Enrico's pasta sauce is actually his **mother's** recipe. *(Enrico may own the sauce but the recipe belongs to his mother.)*

2. To indicate an omission in letters for contracted words and numbers

   He'll seat you when we call your number. *(he will)*

   August '03 was a difficult time for me. *(2003)*

3. To create certain plurals in special situations

   1960's furniture style is now **2006's** chic. *(the furniture of the 1960s is currently popular)*

   I noticed he misspells words ending in **ph's** and **f's**. *(marks the particular words)*

Note: To form possession in a word that already ends in *–s,* add the apostrophe after the existing *–s* or add an apostrophe and another *–s.*

The Sparks' new car rides like a dream. –OR– The Sparks's new car rides like a dream.

Misusing Apostrophes

- When two or more subjects are possessive, always place the apostrophe with the last subject before the verb.

  Robert and Caitlin**'s** vacation was very memorable. *(The vacation belongs to both.)*

  If Robert and Caitlin went on separate vacations:

  Robert**'s** and Caitlin**'s** vacation**s** **were** very memorable. *(Each possesses a vacation.)*

  The **1960s** was a time of turbulence. *(There is nothing to possess or contract here.)*

- When forming the possessive case of personal pronouns, do not use apostrophes.

  He bought h**is** shirt at the concert.   NOT   He bought **his's** shirt at the concert.

  The book has lost **its** cover.   NOT   The book has lost **it's** cover.

Quotation Marks for Quoting, Dialogue, Titles

Quotation marks indicate dialogue that has been spoken, written, or thought; mark certain titles; and set apart words used in unique or special ways.

- Quoting written, thought, or spoken wording

  Katherine Hepburn once said, "A lady always knows when to leave a party."

  About Hepburn's quote I always think, "That advice could save many a young girl's reputation."

  In his paper about underage drinking Brian wrote: "Ladies, don't be the last to leave the party. You might get in trouble."

If the quotation is in the middle of a sentence, use comma tags.

  "A lady," Katherine Hepburn once declared, "always knows when to leave a party."

If the quotation begins the sentence

  "A lady always knows when to leave a party," observed Katherine Hepburn.

If the quotation ends with an exclamation point or question mark, use that instead of the comma, and continue the ending in lower case.

  "What do you mean I could get in trouble by staying late?" asked Tess.

- Quoting prose and poetry

If quoting a line of prose or of poetry, place it within quotation marks.

  In *Middlesex* Jeffrey Eugenides writes, "In the same way, I would like to imagine my brother and me, floating together since the world's beginning on our raft of eggs."

  "How do I love thee, let me count the ways."

For any directly quoted prose or poetry over four lines, omit quotation marks and set off the passage by double indentation from the left margin. For more information, see Chapter 17, "Writing the Research Essay."

- Quoting titles

Titles of poems, articles in magazines and journals, newspapers, book chapters, episodes of television or radio programs, and song titles are all quoted.

Larry Doyle's "I Am Afraid I Have Some Bad News" that is printed in this week's *The New Yorker* evokes satire to prove his point.

Eugenides's first chapter is called "The Silver Spoon."

Do you remember Nickelback's song, "Too Bad"?

- Specially used words

Occasionally—and this technique should be used very sparingly—writers emphasize certain words to evoke sarcasm, satire, disbelief, or other unusual emotions.

He claimed he was "a nice guy" just before killing his family.

A four-page summary is hardly "research" if you ask me.

Punctuating Quotes

- When ending the quotation, place the punctuation inside the quotation.

  Larry Doyle wrote "I Am Afraid I Have Some Bad News."

- Final semicolons and colons go **outside** the quotation marks.

  Sure, I remember the song "Too Bad"; in fact, I just bought the CD yesterday.

- Quotations with question marks, exclamation points, and dashes

If the mark is a part of the quotation, place it **inside** quotation marks. If not, place the mark **outside** of the quotation.

"What do you mean?" he growled.

Did I loan you my copy of "Chapter 9"?

Dashes, Parentheses, Ellipses

- Dashes, which are two hyphens that word processors convert to a solid line, operate like commas within a sentence to mark off **nonessential information** to clarify, explain, expand, demonstrate, or supplement. Unlike the comma, the dash calls attention to the material. However, like parentheses and ellipses, dashes should be used very sparingly if at all in college writing.

  When we arrived at the emergency room—and I am not exaggerating—the place looked like a bomb had exploded.

- Parentheses also set off nonessential material for the purpose of calling more attention to clarify, explain, expand, demonstrate, or supplement.

  In some sections of rural Ohio (and I mean very rural) people have no indoor plumbing.

  You can find numerous accounts of these conditions (see Huff, Chatham, and Burke).

- The ellipses is a set of three periods with single spaces between them (. . .). Instead of adding information like dashes and parentheses, ellipses stand in for omitted passages the author removes for brevity.

  "A parlour or a drawing-room,–a library opening into a garden,–a garden with an alcove in it,–a street, or the piazza of Covent-garden, does well enough in a scene;" remarked Charles Lamb in "On the Tragedies of Shakspeare" [sic]

  converted to read:

  "A parlour . . . a library . . . a street . . . does well enough in a scene;" remarked Charles Lamb in "On the Tragedies of Shakspeare" [sic]

Technology Toolbox

Inserting Page Numbers, Headers, and Footers

Paginating your papers helps you and your professors keep track of your work. In your word processing program, go to "Insert," then choose "Page Numbers." From there you can choose to have the numbers displayed at the top (Header) or bottom (Footer). You can choose alpha or numeric or Roman numerals, and in the advanced options you may include text information.

Level 1

Name_____ **Date**_____

DIRECTIONS Add colons in the sentences that need them.

SAMPLE

Items to have when stranded on a desert island: my cell phone to get rescued, books to read while I waited, and plenty of food and water.

Items to have when stranded on a desert island include my cell phone to get rescued, books to read while I waited, and plenty of food and water.

1. My English professor has several pet peeves people who arrive late to class, who come unprepared, and who do not participate in class.

2. Recently I learned some great suggestions about safety never open the door to a stranger, never leave a purse or wallet near a front door or window, and always lock your car door before starting the engine.

3. My mother has a drawer for each child containing our baby pictures, artwork we did as kids, and some of our assignments.

4. In Ralph Ellison's *The Invisible Man* the main character reflects at the end of the novel "Perhaps to lose a sense of *where* you are implies the danger of losing a sense of *who* you are."

5. These are the items I need in order to register for an email account my driver's license, my class schedule, and my student identification card.

6. I am allergic to several important drugs penicillin, codeine, and aspirin.

7. Cleo's favorite activities sleeping, chasing Cheshire, and sitting on my lap.

8. Great fairy tale lines include "Once upon a time," "Thus it was said," and "They lived happily ever after."

9. Put together a roadside emergency kit and include a blanket, flares, a flashlight, fresh batteries, and some water.

Level 1

Name_____   Date_____

DIRECTIONS Add semicolons after the main clauses in the sentences that need them.

SAMPLE

Dale Chihuly is most known for his brilliant glasswork however he has done much more than simply create art.

Dale Chihuly is most known for his brilliant glasswork; however he has done much more than simply create art.

1. Chihuly became an art student studying blown glass in the early 1960s that was a time when the glass movement was very high.

2. In 1965 he enrolled in the first hot glass program in the U.S. at University of Wisconsin there he began experimenting with many new materials.

3. Since graduating and honing his craft, Chihuly has become known for glass art that experiments with color pieces that can be as small as a paperweight or as large as a room and work that can be displayed indoors as well as outdoors.

4. Some glass-blown pieces are hand formed by the artist in other cases Chihuly blows them into "optic molds" to achieve a different effect.

5. He gathers his inspiration from nature often his upbringing in the Tacoma, Washington figures into his designs.

6. His outdoor garden pieces portray a union between glass and nature reflect the similarities between naturally created landscaping and corresponding glass interpretations as some critics believe, demonstrate the artist's desire to create pieces that are actually glass.

7. To see some of these amazing glass garden interpretations requires visiting such museums like Garfield Park Conservatory in Chicago, Illinois the Franklin Park Conservatory in Columbus, Ohio the Atlanta Botanical Gardens in Atlanta, Georgia and Kew Gardens, London, England.

Level 1

Name_____ **Date**_____

DIRECTIONS Correct the punctuation problems in the following sentences.

SAMPLE

I wondered why I was sent here?   *I wondered why I was sent here.*

1. Actually, the Senate is meeting right now!

2. So in summation, were we right to invade Kuwait.

3. I got tickets to see the Duhks tonight!!!!

4. What are you planning to do about your grade in this class.

5. Hey, you just dropped that weight on my foot?

6. So I was wondering if you would like to go out on a date tomorrow night?

7. Can you, should, you, will you please remember to buy your father a card?!

8. Help, I have fallen and I can't get up.

9. Isn't this lamp that goes on and off when I clap my hands funny!

10. Enrique likes anything retro, so do you think he will like the lamp.

11. Shhh. I can't hear myself think around here!

12. I was amazed when the crowd began screaming, "Encore. More. Encore!"

13. Since you waited this long to see the band, what is one more week!

14. What do you mean you wrecked my car????

Level 1

Name_____ **Date**_____

DIRECTIONS Correct all errors in the following sentences to form proper possessive cases, contractions, and plurals, and then correct the error in the blank to the right.

SAMPLE

The 1990's was a decade about the individual.   _____1990s_____

1. Dr. Clarks' lecture begins promptly at 5:00.   _____

2. Her class's will also attend the lecture so get there early.   _____

3. The guest speaker's discussion about childrens' literature is terrific.   _____

4. I have not heard her speak since the 1980's when she was in school.   _____

5. Its almost time for Ms. Smiths' students to take their's seats.   _____

6. Speaker series's like these are great for our university   _____

7. Dr. Snow's sitting two rows down from our's.   _____

8. The childrens' conditions during the novel are appalling.   _____

9. The speakers emotions became obvious when she read their stories.   _____

10. Obviously, in the 1860's child labor laws were non-existent.   _____

11. That centurys laws in general protected big business and not individuals.   _____

12. Their's are the stories we need to remember so horrors like that die
    forever.   _____

13. This notebook someone left is either her's or Jessica's.   _____

14. I'm glad we attended tonights lecture even if the story's were hard to hear. _____

Level 1

Name_____ Date_____

DIRECTIONS For each type of punctuation or situation specified below, write a correctly punctuated sentence.

SAMPLE

Ellipses

When President Kennedy declared, "Ask not what your country can do for you . . ." he
was trying to instill political service as a valuable trait in every American.

1. A quotation using a song title

   _____

2. Dashes

   _____

3. Parentheses

   _____

4. A quotation using ellipses

   _____

5. Ellipses

   _____

6. A quotation from a famous person

   _____

7. A quotation using a question and parentheses

   _____

Level 2

Name _____ **Date** _____

DIRECTIONS The following paragraph uses colons, semicolons, end punctuation, apostrophes, quotation marks, dashes, parentheses, brackets, and ellipses incorrectly. Rewrite the paragraph with correct punctuation.

Since she was a little girl; Carrie has been interested in math: now she is going to graduate school (and will graduate in the mid 2000's) to become an engineer. As an engineer—Carries' work will focus on light refraction in computer software—her mother Carolyn is amazed that Carrie can raise three children; [Megan, Hunter, and Olivia]; and keep a 4.0 GPA . . . Carries' sisters—Shannon, Anne Marie, and Cindy help Carrie whenever they can: still . . . trying to balance school and responsibilities is hard!

When her Aunt Cindy: who her sister was named after asked Carrie how she handles everything Carries response was: "Its hard but I like what Im doing and I can make a difference some day." Whats easy to see when talking to Carrie is her passion for math and who would'nt support her in her quest to follow her passion!

_____

_____

_____

_____

_____

_____

_____

_____

_____

_____

_____

_____

Constructing Basic Sentences

The Thomson Handbook, **Chapters 33, 36**

The Sentence

In its most basic form, a **simple sentence** is a complete grammatical expression, which contains a **simple subject** and a **simple predicate.** Together, those two parts **express a complete thought.**

> I ate. *(The thought is complete and the reader needs no further information.)*
>
> I *(This thought is incomplete. I what?)*

A **simple subject** consists of a noun or pronoun.

A **simple predicate** consists of the intransitive verb or verb phrase that performs or describes an action. An **intransitive verb** does not need an object or additional wording to express complete meaning.

A **complete thought** is a group of words that expresses an action completed by someone or something and makes sense without additional information.

Simple sentences may be written in five basic combinations:

1. Subject + Intransitive Verb
2. Subject + Intransitive Verb + Direct Object
3. Subject + Intransitive Verb + Direct Object + Object Complement
4. Subject + Intransitive Verb + Subject Complement
5. Subject + Transitive Verb + Indirect Object + Direct Object

Combination 1: Subject + Intransitive Verb

> I ate. *(The intransitive verb ate needs no additional wording to express the action.)*
>
> S   V
> Jack needs food. *(A subject, in this case an animate being which could be a person or an animal, requires nourishment. This thought is complete.)*
>
> Jack needs. *(This thought is incomplete because the reader cannot tell what the subject needs.)*
>
> V   S
> Feed the dog. *(complete thought)*

Combination 2: Subject + Transitive Verb + Direct Object

> S   V   DO
> Gene cut the grass.

A **transitive verb** requires an object to complete the meaning. In this sentence *cut* is transitive because it needs a **direct object** to demonstrate where or who is affected by the verb's action. In this case, the grass is affected by the verb *cut*.

   S   V   DO

Pam baked an apple pie. *(Pam performed an act by baking and performed that act on an apple pie.)*

Combination 3: Subject + Intransitive Verb + Direct Object + Object Complement

A sentence incorporating a word or group of words that describes or renames the direct object contains an **object complement.**

        S   V   OC

The old lighthouse was a beacon for sailors. *(Here beacon describes the lighthouse.)*

     S   V   DO   OC

The hikers decided the trail was difficult. (Difficult *defines or describes the trail.*)

Combination 4: Subject + Intransitive Verb + Subject Complement

This combination's sentences contain a subject, a **linking verb,** which links or joins the subject to the complement, and the **subject complement,** the words or phrases describing or renaming the subject.

      S   LV   SC

Her assignment was terrific. (Terrific *describes the assignment.*)

   S   LV SC

Roark is happy living in his new house. (Happy *describes Roark.*)

Combination 5: Subject + Transitive Verb + Indirect Object + Direct Object

In a sentence containing a **direct object** (showing where the action is directed and who or what the action involves), there can also be an **indirect object** (showing to whom or what the action was done). The **indirect object** precedes the **direct object** and is usually associated with verbs that indicate giving or communicating like *give, bring, tell, show, take,* or *offer.*

    S   V   IO   DO

Roark planted Helena a garden. *(For whom was the garden planted? The garden was planted for Helena, so Roark gave her the garden.)*

     S   V   IO   DO

The runner passed the baton to her teammate. *(To whom was the baton passed? The runner passed or gave the baton to her teammate.)*

Correcting Sentence Fragment Writing Habits

Two habits writers get into that create fragments are writing **appositive fragments** and **prepositional phrase fragments.** For the first type of fragment, the second sentence, the appositive fragment, describes or modifies the previous sentence.

Appositive fragment:

He planted flowers and vegetables. <u>Sunflowers, asters, tomatoes, and cucumbers.</u> *(The second sentence describes what kind of flowers and vegetables he planted.)*

Revised:

He planted flowers and vegetables, such as sunflowers, asters, tomatoes, and cucumbers.

A **prepositional phrase fragment** is a phrase that also modifies the previous sentence.

Prepositional fragment:

I could hear your phone conversation. <u>Through the door.</u>

Revised:

I could hear your phone conversation through the door.

The Clause

A **clause** consists of a subject and a predicate but is not a sentence; it is either an **independent** or a **dependent clause.**

An **independent clause** is a complete thought and can stand alone as a **complete sentence.**

A **dependent** or **subordinate clause** does not express a complete thought, so it must always be combined with an independent clause to form a **complete sentence.**

Dependent clauses are **noun, adjective, or adverb clauses.**

When writers try to make a dependent clause stand alone, they create **sentence fragments,** which you will study in detail in Chapter 41 of *The Thomson Handbook* and in the next chapter of this workbook.

Carol has a saltwater aquarium. *(independent clause that expresses a complete thought)*

INDEP. CLAUSE   DEPEN. CLAUSE *(NOT A COMPLETE THOUGHT)*

<u>Carol has a saltwater aquarium</u> *because she likes the fish better.*

Adjective or Relative Clauses

These phrases modify nouns or pronouns, always follow the nouns or pronouns they modify, and begin with a relative pronoun (**which, that, what, whatever, who, whose, whom, whomever, whoever**, or the adverbs **where or when**).

Saltwater aquariums, **which are more difficult to care for than freshwater ones**, can be very rewarding. *(The clause modifies the noun* aquarium.*)*

Carol, who recently added some Green Mandarin Goby fish to her aquarium, is ready to buy some live coral. *(The clause modifies the proper noun* Carol.*)*

Adverb Clauses

Adverb clauses modify verbs, adjectives, adverbs, and independent clauses. Adverb clauses are always introduced by a **subordinating conjunction,** which is a word that joins together a dependent clause and an independent clause (*because, although, while, whereas, since, as*). Adverb clauses also answer how, where, when, why, and to what extent.

Because saltwater fish are very expensive, Carol must clean her tank often. *(clause explains why Carol must clean the tank)*

Carol has had to budget her spending, **since she started her saltwater tank.** (*clause explains why Carol has had to be careful with her money*)

Noun Clauses

These clauses work as subjects, direct or indirect objects, predicate nouns, object of a preposition, object complement, or appositive to a subject or object. These clauses usually begin with *that, what, where, when, who, whom, which, whose, how, why,* or *whether.*

NOUN CLAUSE   VB

Why Carol spends so much on her tank is a mystery to her roommates.

VB   OBJECT OF VERB *ASKED*

They asked **whether or not she could afford the bills.**

Technology Toolbox

Checking for Sentence Fragments

Your word processing program probably contains a grammar checker, which is equipped to find sentence fragments. When the checker thinks it has spotted a fragment or incomplete sentence, you will see a green squiggly line. When you right-click on the line, the program will suggest that you revise. However, this feature, like all in these programs, is not foolproof! The way you construct a sentence might make the program think your sentence is complete when it is not. If you're unsure, always double-check the rules in *The Thomson Handbook.*

Level 1

Name_____ Date_____

DIRECTIONS In the following sentences underline the subject once, the verb twice, and circle the predicate.

SAMPLE

Dot wanted (a new car.)

1. Karen and Jim said they would help Dot.

2. First, Dot decided she wanted a hybrid car.

3. Jim did some online research about the kinds of hybrids available.

4. Dot, Karen, and Jim read Jim's research carefully because buying a car is a big decision.

5. Though they were divided, all three liked the Honda Civic hybrid the best.

6. Dot chose two dealerships to visit.

7. At the first dealership the salesperson showed Dot, Jim, and Karen three models of the Civic.

8. Dot thanked the salesperson and left because she wanted a better selection.

9. At the second dealership Dot found many choices.

10. Then Dot drove the car she liked most to make sure she was purchasing wisely.

11. Next, the salesperson began the negotiations such as price and car options.

12. This part of the car buying process is probably the longest and hardest.

13. After several hours of haggling, Dot signed her contract and purchased her brand new, silver Civic sedan.

Level 1

Name_____ **Date**_____

DIRECTIONS In the following sentences underline the subject once, the verb twice, and label any direct objects, indirect objects, subject complements, and object complements.

SAMPLE

                                                    sc
  The banana is one of the most important fruits in the human diet.

1. Originally from Malaysia, bananas are the world's most popular fruit.

2. Alexander the Great loved the banana from his first bite.

3. Alexander introduced bananas to the Western world.

4. One large banana contains about 600 mg. of potassium.

5. After a race volunteers give athletes bananas to eat.

6. Melanie loves bananas that are just ripe.

7. Most people do not like mushy bananas.

8. The track team chose bananas as their favorite food.

9. Banana smoothies are also nutritional.

10. Janet made the track team a huge batch of smoothies.

11. Joanne bakes banana bread from scratch.

12. Elvis Presley loved fried peanut butter and banana sandwiches.

13. Loaded with potassium and vitamins, the banana is the perfect fruit.

Level 1

Name_____ Date_____

DIRECTIONS The following sentences contain errors in appositive and prepositional phrase fragments. Correct each sentence in the space provided.

SAMPLE

The Peace Corps was born into service in 1960. <u>Because of President John F. Kennedy's call to Americans to work for peace in developing countries.</u>

Because President John F. Kennedy asked Americans to help work for peace in developing countries, the Peace Corps was created in 1960.

1. Actually, Kennedy was speaking to students from the University of Michigan. At the time.

2. The Corps is dedicated to spreading world peace and friendship between countries. In place of hostility and mistrust.

3. Over 182,000 people have served in the Peace Corps since 1960. In places like Latin America, North Africa, the Middle East, Eastern Europe, and Asia.

4. In spite of changes in the world today. Today's volunteers work to many of the same goals as their predecessors.

5. According to actual members. The chance to immerse themselves in another culture and help is an amazing gift and opportunity.

Level 1

Name_____ Date_____

DIRECTIONS Read the groups of words below and mark in the space to the right whether they are independent or dependent clauses.

SAMPLE

    A rose by any other name.   *Dependent*

1. Because I could not stop for death. _____

2. It stopped for me. _____

3. These are the days. _____

4. To remember. _____

5. Never before and never since. _____

6. I promise. _____

7. Will the whole world be as warm as this. _____

8. And as you feel it, you'll know it's true. _____

9. That you are blessed and lucky. _____

10. It's true that you are touched by something. _____

11. That will grow and bloom in you. _____

12. These are the days you might. _____

13. Fill with laughter until you break. _____

14. And when you do. _____

15. You'll know how it was meant to be. _____

Level 2

Name_____ Date_____

DIRECTIONS Each sentence contains independent and dependent clauses. Underline the main subject once, the verb twice, and circle the main clause. In the blank to the right, identify the clause.

SAMPLE

Astronaut Jim Lovell, who commanded the Apollo 13 flight, did not get
to walk on the moon at that time.   *adj. clause*

1. The Apollo 13 mission, which seemed doomed from the start, was
   successful because the astronauts returned alive.   _____

2. The crew was to land in the Fra Mauro region of the moon, where
   they would gather samples to bring back to Earth.   _____

3. After an explosion occurred that crippled their spacecraft, NASA
   decided which was more important.   _____

4. At the last minute Jack Swigert replaced Ken Mattingly who allegedly
   contracted the measles.   _____

5. Because Ken Mattingly did not have the measles, he was able to help
   ground control come up with answers to the carbon monoxide
   problem in the craft.   _____

6. Captain Jim Lovell, who had more experience in the Apollo program
   than the rest of the crew, kept a cool head during dangerous times.   _____

7. Stunned after they saw the damage, the crew was able to photograph
   the ailing command module before releasing it into space.   _____

8. That it was even operational was one of many strange occurrences in
   the mission.   _____

9. The Service Module, where the oxygen, water, and power sources were
   stored, was also to house the astronauts for most of the journey.   _____

Level 2

Name_____ **Date**_____

DIRECTIONS The following rough draft needs revision to remove the sentence fragments. In some cases a verb is missing, and in others a subject. Underline all sentence fragments. Then revise the paragraph into a second draft worthy of submitting. You may rewrite sentences and you should work on improving the flow between sentences with transitions.

SAMPLE

Collecting is a hobby that has been a part of American heritage. <u>For a long time.</u>

For centuries many Americans have been collectors of memorabilia.

Practically every family contains at least one collector. Stamps, coins, music. Are examples. Others collect figurines of specific characters. Like pigs or Elvis for example. Why do people collect? As research shows. There are many reasons people spend money on their hobbies.

Stamp collectors learn about major historical events. Famous people also. Such as Martin Luther King, Jr. Hattie McDaniel, and Benjamin Franklin. People who collect books can use their hobbies. However, not the rare books. Which are expensive and should not be handled. Collecting can be very expensive. But also cheap. Collecting artwork or weapons is an example of an expensive collection. Whereas recipes from the paper are inexpensive. Collectors will tell you often the price is not an issue. Satisfaction matters.

I used to think blueberries were okay; however, now I love them. *(semicolon and transitional phrase)*

Though I used to think blueberries were okay, now I love them. *(subordinated the first clause)*

A **fused sentence** contains even less than a sentence with a comma splice. A fused sentence joins two or more independent clauses without punctuation or conjunctions.

Fused sentence:

I love fresh blueberries on my cereal I also eat them on ice cream.

Revised:

I love fresh blueberries on my cereal**, and** I also eat them on ice cream. *(comma + coordinating conjunction)*

I love fresh blueberries on my cereal**;** I also eat them on ice cream. *(a semicolon to separate)*

I love fresh blueberries on my cereal**; however,** I also eat them on ice cream. *(a semicolon and a transitional phrase)*

As much as I love fresh blueberries on my cereal**,** I also eat them on ice cream. *(subordinate the first clause)*

Technology Toolbox

Highlight Potential Errors

When writing a draft, turn off your Spelling and Grammar Checker. When you think you might have written a sentence containing errors, select the Highlight tool and mark the sentence in question. You can change the Highlight color to reflect different questions, thus color coding your paper so you can go back and find your place easily. This markup system is especially helpful when you take your paper to your school's writing center or have a friend read it.

Level 1

Name_____ **Date**_____

DIRECTIONS The word groups below may or may not be complete sentences. Underline the subject, circle the verb, and in the blank to the right choose whether the sentence is a fragment by writing "frag" or a complete sentence by writing "com." If the sentence is a fragment, list the missing elements (subject, verb, direct object, indirect object).

SAMPLE

My <u>roommate</u> on the golf team.   *frag.–no vb*

1. Karen practices every day.   _____

2. After dinner and before she hits the books.   _____

3. Because she practices so much.   _____

4. No time for laundry or fun.   _____

5. By working so hard on her game can hurt her grades.   _____

6. Because I worry about how she is doing.   _____

7. Which is why I need to sit her down for a talk.   _____

8. For concentrating on sports only got Karen on academic probation.   _____

9. Caring about her future like I do.   _____

10. Although she seems to understand the problem.   _____

11. A serious problem with lots of consequences.   _____

12. Though I think she will listen to reason.   _____

13. To prove she can handle athletics and academics.   _____

Level 1

Name_____ **Date**_____

DIRECTIONS Revise the following word groups from the previous exercise to form a complete paragraph about a student named Karen who has let golf take over her life. The author is you, Karen's roommate. You will need to reorder the sentences to make sense and clarify.

SAMPLE

My <u>roommate</u> on the golf team. *My roommate is on the golf team at school.*

Karen practices every day. After dinner and before she hits the books.

Because she practices so much. No time for laundry or fun. By working so hard on her game can hurt her grades. Because I worry about how she is doing. Which is why I need to sit her down for a talk. For concentrating on sports only got Karen on academic probation. Caring about her future like I do. Although she seems to understand the problem. A serious problem with lots of consequences. Though I think she will listen to reason. To prove she can handle athletics and academics.

_____

_____

_____

_____

_____

_____

_____

_____

_____

_____

_____

_____

Level 1

Name_____ Date_____

DIRECTIONS Read carefully the following passage which contains correct sentences as well as sentence fragments. Underline each fragment, and revise it in the space below by attaching an independent clause that contains the word or group of words being modified.

SAMPLE

In the summer Anne and Taylor must make a choice. <u>Between getting a job and relaxing.</u>

In the summer Anne and Taylor must decide between getting jobs or relaxing.

Each summer is always a dilemma for Anne and her younger brother Taylor. Because they are old enough to work. At Malbon Farm selling homegrown fruits and vegetables. Sometimes Grandad takes Taylor to tennis. Anne to Aunt Vicky's pool with her friends. If they worked, they would not have time for beach and tennis. Although there are days off. When she works at the fruit stand Anne meets new people and sees old friends. Last year she met her boyfriend. Who was with his parents buying vegetables. On slow days Anne reads. Which helps pass the time and keeps her sharp. Taylor feeds the animals in the petting zoo. He loves the goats best. Because they play and try to butt him like one of their own. Ultimately, Anne and Taylor work and play all summer.

_____

_____

_____

_____

_____

_____

_____

_____

_____

_____

Level 1

Name_____ **Date**_____

DIRECTIONS Revise each sentence twice in the spaces provided. First, delete the conjunction or pronoun that makes the clause dependent to turn it into an independent phrase that can stand alone. Second, add to the original dependent clause to make a grammatically complete sentence.

SAMPLE

After it snowed last night.

It snowed last night.

After it snowed last night we went outside for a big snowball fight.

1. Once Elena started her workout.

    a. _____

    b. _____

2. By running on the treadmill for 2 miles

    a. _____

    b. _____

3. Although many prefer free weights

    a. _____

    b. _____

4. David, a certified fitness instructor, who helps Elena with her workouts.

    a. _____

    b. _____

Level 1

Name_____ **Date**_____

DIRECTIONS The following sentences contain comma splices, fused sentences, or both. Revise each sentence in the space below to make it grammatically correct by: creating two separate sentences, by using a coordinating conjunction, or by using a semicolon and conjunction. Make sure you try each revision method at least once.

SAMPLE

American history books have overlooked African American inventors, these important figures must receive their due.

Though history books have overlooked African American inventors, now is the

time for these important figures to receive their due.

Dr. Charles Drew invented the Blood Bank and a way to preserve blood plasma longer, he discovered that plasma stored better than whole blood.

_____

_____

George Crum invented the potato chip, he worked as a chef and tried to please a customer who wanted something different than french fries.

_____

_____

Garrett Morgan invented the gas mask and was the first to patent the traffic light he later made gas masks for the U.S. Army.

_____

_____

Level 1

Name _____ **Date** _____

DIRECTIONS The following sentences contain comma splices, fused sentences, or both. Identify whether the sentence has a comma splice (cs) or is a fused sentence (fs) in the blank to the right.

SAMPLE

A 2006 study reveals the Earth is hotter than it has been in 400 years this confirms that global warming is a reality.   _Fused sentence_

1. The National Academy of Sciences confirms its findings, the Earth has not been as hot as this in perhaps 2000 years.   _____

2. "Human activities are responsible for much of the warming" the scientists confirmed this statement in their 155 page report.   _____

3. The Earth grew 1 degree hotter in the 20th century, this may not seem like much but that counts for massive changes in animal and plant life.   _____

4. Other scientists confirmed the terrible hurricane season in 2005 was due to rising temperatures, many earlier said the season was due to climate patterns.   _____

5. Studies find, carbon dioxide and methane the greenhouse gasses are most responsible.   _____

6. Records show from 1 A.D. to 1850 volcano eruptions created most greenhouse gasses, from 1850 to today pollution has been the biggest culprit.   _____

7. The study confirms what scientists have been warning us about we need to take measures to greatly reduce greenhouse emissions and protect our planet.   _____

Level 1

Name_____ **Date**_____

DIRECTIONS Underline the comma splices and fused sentences in the following paragraph and indicate whether the sentence contains a comma splice (cs) or is a fused sentence (fs) at the end. Use the strategies shown in the chapter to correct the errors in the space provided below.

SAMPLE

(fs)

<u>Jeanne loves sunflowers they remind her of the beach.</u>

<u>*Jeanne loves sunflowers because they remind her of the beach.*</u>

    Every summer Jeanne's family went to Bethany Beach, Delaware, they had a cottage right on the water. Their cottage was next to Shannon's, each summer Jeanne and Shannon hung out together. On the other side was Mary's family's cottage, she and Jeanne and Shannon were inseparable all summer. Some days the kids would play in the water their parents would read and swim with them too. Everyone learned how to surf on this beat up old long board they kept at the cottage, each kid taking a turn. Some days everyone rented bikes on the boardwalk. Jeanne, Shannon, and Mary usually got ice cream the other kids spent their money in the arcade. At night the families either joined each other at one family's cottage or went out, there were so many restaurants to choose from.

_____

_____

_____

_____

_____

_____

_____

_____

_____

_____

_____

Level 2

Name_____ **Date**_____

DIRECTIONS The following paragraph contains fragments, comma splices, and fused sentences. Revise and rewrite a corrected version in the space provided. Don't forget to use correct punctuation!

College is a great way to meet people from backgrounds other than your own especially if you move from your hometown to an unfamiliar area and need to make a whole new set of friends which happens to most freshmen anyway. Since the United States is a melting pot culture; meeting people from diverse backgrounds is important. Becoming culturally aware; helps us understand different viewpoints on issues. Because it is important to recognize other valid opinions. For example Margarita is from Bulgaria, she came to the U.S. to earn a degree get a job and live in America. In college she met Enrico. From Italy. Margarita does not speak Italian, Enrico does not speak Bulgarian. The both speak English and have made lots of friends in America. Mark's family is from the Philippines and he says people constantly ask him if he is Japanese, he sometimes gets tired of feeling like he needs to educate people but at the same time he is pleased that some are interested in being correct and not just assuming if he looks Asian he is either Chinese or Japanese.

_____

_____

_____

_____

_____

_____

_____

_____

_____

_____

_____

Simple to Complex Sentence Patterns

The Thomson Handbook, **Chapters 36, 37**

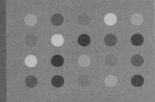

As you begin writing grammatically correct complex sentences in this chapter, you will need to draw upon the knowledge you gained specifically in Chapter 8, because complex sentences utilize independent and dependent clauses to **coordinate** and **subordinate** ideas expressed in the sentence.

This chapter is designed to help writers develop common strategies as well as creativity to move away from writing only shorter sentences. Though conciseness is a point we will cover later, concise sentences are not the same as short sentences. A string of short sentences that do not have longer ones interspersed for variety becomes too monotonous for the reader to follow:

> My friend Shannon is Irish. Her birthday is March 18. That is one day after St. Patrick's Day. She always has a birthday party. Sometimes her party is on March 17. I always wear green on her birthday.

The writer tries to demonstrate how unfortunate it is that her Irish friend's birthday falls one day after St. Patrick's Day, and how the friend still manages to celebrate her birthday and the holiday at the same time. Too bad the monotonous sentence pattern detracts from the message by forcing the reader to concentrate less on the meaning and more on the style.

Remember: Creating complex sentences requires you to connect your ideas, give instructions to your readers about meaning, and organize information according to importance.

Here is the same set of sentences revised with *and,* the most common of the **coordinating conjunctions.**

> My friend Shannon's birthday is March 18, **and** she is Irish. Sometimes she celebrates her birthday on St. Patrick's Day, **and** I always wear green.

In this chapter we will concentrate on establishing variety between shorter and longer thoughts. First, we discuss the two ways to extend your sentences that you learned in Chapter 8.

Coordination

Writers link two independent clauses (complete sentences) by a inserting a **coordinating conjunction.** Think of **coordination** like a balance or scales where the ideas in the independent clauses are equal.

> **Two choppy sentences:**
> Shannon's birthday is March 18. She just missed St. Patrick's Day by one day.

Choppy sentences linked by coordination: **(linking through a** coordinating conjunction**)**

Shannon's birthday is March 18 **and** she just missed St. Patrick's Day by one day.

Shannon's birthday is March 18, **so** she just missed St. Patrick's Day by one day.

Shannon celebrates her birthday on March 18, **or** she has her party on the 17th.

Shannon's birthday is on March 18, **yet** she often celebrates on the 17th.

Shannon had a birthday party on March 17, **but** her birthday is actually the 18th.

As explained in Chapter 8, always put a comma before the coordinating conjunction that joins two independent clauses.

How the Coordinating Conjunctions Establish Meaning or Give Instruction

Choosing the least correct coordinating conjunction can make a mess of your sentences, so be sure you understand what each suggests to the reader:

And connects as in addition to, part of a list or sequence, or similar ideas

But and *yet* connect two contrasting ideas or show cause

Or or *nor* connect two dissimilar or separate ideas; indicate a choice or alternative

So shows how the second idea is the result or effect of the preceding idea

For shows cause

Subordination

Whereas **coordination** links two independent clauses with a **coordinating conjunction,** **subordination** is the process in which authors join an independent clause with a **dependent clause.**

The strategy in using subordination involves ranking your ideas so the more important ones are located in the independent clause and the less important ideas are found in the dependent clause. The conjunctive adverbs *although, however,* and *therefore* are often key transitions to less important ideas.

Choppy:

Antwan signed up for a cooking class. The class is located at the YMCA on Warwick Blvd.

Subordinate:

Antwan signed up for a cooking class although it is offered at the YMCA on Warwick Blvd. *(The main idea is that Antwan is taking a cooking class, not where the class is located.)*

Choppy:

For the next four weeks Antwan will learn how to cook healthy dishes. He will cook pasta with marinara one week. The next week he will try burritos. The third week he will grill chicken. The fourth week he will learn how to broil fish.

Subordinate:

For the next four weeks Antwon will learn how to cook healthy dishes; therefore, pasta with marinara, burritos, grilled chicken, and broiled fish are part of the class.

Sentences which give information about time, a place, extra descriptions, or explain a cause/effect situation need a subordinate/dependent phrase.

Choppy:

Danielle, Kate, and Maggie tried to register early for classes, and they accidentally overloaded the online system. *(The sentence fails to connect the girls' action with the effect or consequence it created.)*

Subordinate:

By trying to register for classes early, Danielle, Kate, and Maggie accidentally overloaded the online registration system. *(explains that their attempt to access the online registration system before the correct time caused an overload to occur)*

Choppy:

Danielle, Kate, and Maggie worried they would not get the right classes, get the right times, or have to find replacements, so they tried to register early.

Subordinate:

By trying to register for classes early, Danielle, Kate, and Maggie wanted to get the right classes, schedule the right times, or have time to find substitutions.

Make sure to place a comma after the adverbial clause if it precedes an independent clause.

Because they were worried about their schedules, Danielle, Kate, and Maggie tried to register early.

Although they did not think they could access the system, Danielle, Kate, and Maggie tried to register early.

Because of their blunder, the university's online class registration system crashed.

Transitional Words or Phrases

In addition to joining two independent clauses with **coordinating conjunctions,** you can also use **transitional words** and **phrases.** Always precede the transitional phrase with a semicolon and follow it with a comma.

Remember: Transitional words and phrases signal a relationship between the words and ideas, so choose carefully from the list below.

Choppy:

Wilma and Evelyn usually eat July 4th dinner with Bill and Carol. This year Bill and Carol are going out of town.

Revised with transitional word:

Wilma and Evelyn usually eat July 4th dinner with Bill and Carol; **however,** this year Bill and Carol are going out of town. *(indicates a shift in habit or process)*

Choppy:

Whenever possible, Ann and Alan like to fly home. With two boys, this can be difficult.

Revised with transitional phrase:

Whenever possible, Ann and Alan like to fly home; **on the other hand,** with two boys, this can be difficult. *(shows a contrast between what they like and reality)*

<u>Common Transitional Words and Phrases</u>
<u>or</u>
<u>Directing Traffic with Words</u>

Show Connection, Sequence, Addition
and, also, besides, first/second/third, furthermore, in addition, too

Show Time

after, at first, at the same time, before, earlier, finally, in the meantime, later, meanwhile, next, now, soon, then, until

Show Comparison

also, in comparison, likewise, similarly

Show Contrast

although, but, despite, even though, however, instead, nevertheless, nonetheless, on the contrary, on the other hand, still, yet

Show Example

chiefly, for example, for instance, specifically, thus

Show Focus

after all, indeed, in fact, in other words, specifically

Show Conclusion or Summary

as a result, consequently, in conclusion, in other words, to summarize, therefore, thus, to conclude

Show Concession

admittedly, certainly, granted, naturally, of course

Show Cause or Effect

accordingly, as a result, because, consequently, hence, since, so, then, therefore

Correlative Conjunctions

These connecting words and phrases are easy to recognize because they always occur in pairs and draw relationships between grammatically equal elements.

Neither Kristin **nor** Kate wanted to go to the beach that day.

Just as Robert attended ECU, **so** will Caitlin.

Correlative Conjunctions

both . . . and	either . . . or	not only . . . but also
just as . . . so	whether . . . or	neither . . . nor

Semicolons and Colons

Semicolons

As you learned in Chapter 6, semicolons can join independent clauses to create a complex or compound sentence, and you do not need a conjunction. Remember, the clauses must be closely related or the second one must build off the first to make sense to your readers.

Mike applied for journalism intern positions for the summer; he wanted a position in the music industry.

Many of the 2006 graduates already had job leads; others were going on to graduate school.

Colons

You may also use a colon to join two independent clauses and create a compound sentence. However, this strategy is not typical and should be used sparingly.

The crowd left before the end of the game: the outcome was certain.

Carol and Peter fell in love with their shaggy dog at first sight: they named him Wookie.

Technology Toolbox

Checking for Sentence Errors

Let your word processor warn you about potential trouble when you expand simple sentences. After writing a rough draft, turn on your Spelling and Grammar function and see if the program picks up any sentence issues. You will typically get an explanatory message like "Fragment (consider revising)" which informs you of the error. Cross reference that error with *The Thomson Handbook* and exercises you did in *The Thomson Handbook Workbook*. If you want more information and exercises, search the Web using a specific keyword search like "sentence fragment." Soon your writing will be free of errors!

Level 1

Name_____ **Date**_____

DIRECTIONS Choose the coordinating conjunction that makes the most sense to improve the following paragraph.

SAMPLE

> *The Bad Beginning* is the first of the Lemony Snicket series, _and or so_ it introduces the Baudelaire children and the tragedy.

In *The Bad Beginning* the narrator introduces readers to the Baudelaire children _____ this description sets up the remaining 11 novels surrounding Violet, Klaus, and Sunny Baudelaire. We learn before we meet the children that they will always be surrounded by bad luck _____ it seems as though misfortune is their nature. The narrator explains, "I'm sorry to tell you this, _____ that is how the story goes."

In the first chapter Violet, Klaus, and Sunny are at the beach _____ Mr. Poe shows up unexpectedly. The weather is foggy and dismal _____ the reader gets the sense that something is wrong. The children are not ready for such horrible news _____ is the reader. He explains that their house burned to the ground _____ so did their parents. The children learn that the fire was suspicious _____ much drama begins to build about their own safety. The reader and the children foresee trouble when Count Olaf adopts them _____ there is nothing to do but hope they survive his evil ways. To help you understand Olaf's sinister nature, he has a single eyebrow _____ he has a tattoo of an eye on his ankle. I would tell you how things end, _____ that might spoil your fun!

Level 1

Name_____ Date_____

DIRECTIONS Revise the sentence clusters to feature a subordinating clause and an independent clause. Combine the sentences either with conjunctive adverbs or without them.

SAMPLE

Impressionism is a major art movement still popular today. It began in the late 19th century in France.

Although Impressionism began in the late 19th century in France, it is still

a major art movement today.

1. The first painters in the movement included Monet, Renoir, Pissarro, Sisley, and Bazille. Degas, Cezanne, and Manet joined the movement later.

2. The artists shared a common vision and artistic strategy. They attempted to capture realistic scenes using experiments with light and color.

3. Paintings depicting leisure activities of the middle class were popular with the Impressionists. Some depicted café scenes of people talking and eating.

4. Before the Impressionists, painters painted landscapes in studios. Renoir and Monet went into the countryside with their paints and easels to capture realistic images.

5. Often an artist worked on a series of paintings of the same scene or subject. This technique enabled them to demonstrate how light and shadow affected the work.

6. The artists used small paint strokes to record such subtleties involving shadow and light. This technique was initially criticized by the public and art patrons.

7. The small stroke technique allowed the artists to use more color. The use of brighter colors symbolized natural sunlight.

8. The infusion of colors requires the viewer to actively participate in looking at the painting. The viewer mixes the colors instead of passively receiving the image.

9. The Impressionists were interested in interpreting realism. The were not interested in exact reproductions.

Level 1

Name_____ **Date**_____

DIRECTIONS Rewrite the following choppy sentences into a smooth paragraph by using transitional words and phrases to signal direction, help the reader understand, and create flow.

SAMPLE

Scientists found evidence of sea turtles in the Late Jurassic period. The Late Jurassic period was 208 to 144 million years ago.

Scientists found evidence of sea turtles in the Late Jurassic period;

consequently, sea turtles have been around for 144 to 208 million years.

Turtles are reptiles. Reptiles are cold-blooded vertebrates. They have scaly skin. They have lungs so they breathe air. Most reptiles lay eggs. There are two kinds of turtles. One kind has a shell that is connected to its spine. The other is the leatherback. The leatherback's shell is not attached to its skin. The leatherback has leathery skin. Sea turtles like to live in warm water all over the world. They live in shallow waters near the shore, in bays, and in smaller bodies of water. They will travel thousands of miles or sometimes a few to breed and nest. It is hard to know how many turtles there are. Most male and young turtles do not come ashore. Only female turtles come to shore to breed. This makes it difficult for scientists to get an accurate population count. Scientists believe many turtle species are endangered. They believe this because nesting sites are becoming less numerous. Many nesting sites are protected by the state or a wildlife association. Scientists hope to help increase sea turtle populations by tagging adults and protecting nests. This data should show migration patterns and population numbers.

_____

_____

_____

_____

_____

_____

_____

_____

Level 1

Name_____ **Date**_____

DIRECTIONS Rewrite each of the following choppy sentences by writing another simple sentence and joining the two using semicolons and colons to make complex sentences. You may move elements around to rank the main and the subordinate ideas.

SAMPLE

In the summer many people grill outdoors.

People like to grill more in the summertime: the weather is better and it stays lighter longer.

1. In some parts of the country people barbeque and others grill

_____

2. Tomorrow we are having hot dogs and hamburgers

_____

3. Once I grilled a pizza

_____

4. Some partially cook chicken before putting on the grill

_____

5. When grilling corn on the cob you have to be careful

_____

6. The big debate in cooking outdoors is whether to use gas or charcoal

_____

7. Like everything, we each put our personal touches on a cookout

_____

Level 1

Name_____ Date_____

DIRECTIONS Combine the following independent and dependent clause pairs into a compound sentence by using coordination, subordination, transitions, correlative conjunctions, semicolons, or colons.

SAMPLE

Public schools traditionally meet from September to June. This schedule is thought to serve farmers whose children worked the fields.

Although today's public school schedule requires students to meet from

September to June, this system is thought to originally have served the

farmers whose children worked the fields.

1. Some historians dispute the September to June belief. They say 1830s records show that children went to school from December to March and May to August.

   _____

   _____

2. The three-month vacation topic causes great controversy. Many are for it and just as many are against.

   _____

   _____

3. Reasons why against include working parents who cannot stay home during the summer to watch their children, students forget what they learned during long times away from school, and the energy it costs to heat and cool schools even when they are empty.

   _____

   _____

4. Many support the current three-month off system. Because students can work and save money, go on vacations, go to summer schools or camps, or participate in community building programs.

   _____

   _____

5. The three-month summer vacation benefits the school system too. Administrators use the time to repair equipment, thoroughly clean the schools, and order supplies for the upcoming year.

_____

_____

6. In Europe and Asia school years are longer and vacations shorter. European and Asian children spend more hours per day in school.

_____

_____

7. Some American schools have switched to a system of nine weeks of school and three weeks of vacation. Resort areas where student employment is important to the local economy do not like this system.

_____

_____

8. In this debate the students themselves have very little to say. Someone should ask them what they prefer.

_____

_____

9. The argument seems to surround tradition and practicality. Not considering the differences between climates, needs, and purposes of American communities.

_____

_____

Level 2

Name_____ **Date**_____

DIRECTIONS Use the different methods you have learned in this chapter to properly construct compound sentences from the following simple sentences.

The greyhound breed can be traced back through history 8000 years. Probably all domestic dogs descend from this animal. Egyptians worshipped greyhounds. This can be seen in many artworks depicting them as royals. Most pet greyhounds are retired track dogs. These dogs were trained to run races. Most retire after age two. The physical work is grueling.

Pet greyhounds are loyal. They have a few basic needs that are different from other pets. They need enclosed areas. They cannot just run free. Greyhounds need to be trained to use the stairs. They are usually good with children. Many of their former handlers socialized them with children. They are pack animals. Pack animals need an "alpha" member to lead. It is up to the greyhound owner to be the alpha. If not, the greyhound will try to become the house leader. They grow up having never seen other dog species. Trainers and owners say they are highly intelligent.

In addition to great athletic skills greyhounds have keen sight. They have sharp hearing. A greyhound has almost no body fat. This makes them indoor animals. They should never be tied to a leash or left outside for long periods of time. Retired greyhounds as pets are mostly sweet. They can be very curious and love to relax. Many retired hounds have no interest in running. Owners also say they are fast learners and anxious to please.

_____

_____

_____

_____

_____

_____

_____

_____

_____

_____

Parallelism

The Thomson Handbook, Chapter 34

Parallelism in writing requires balance and repetition of equivalent ideas and concepts through similarly phrased words, phrases, clauses, sentences, headings, and titles—even down to the examples used to demonstrate an idea. Lists of items must be similar; nouns need other nouns, verb endings must be the same, gerunds go with gerunds. When done well, we do not notice parallel wording and sentences.

Writing Tip: let the first word, phrase, clause, or element in a series dictate the parallel structure. That way, if you write an unbalanced sentence you can always return to the beginning and correct what follows.

> **A balanced sentence:**
> Sharon likes to prepare Asian noodles, Thai eggrolls, and Indian rice. *(The writer precedes each food with its country of origin.)*

> **An unbalanced sentence:**
> Sharon likes to prepare Asian noodles, eggrolls from Thailand, and rice. *(The writer departs from the pattern by reversing the food item and the country of origin in the second element and leaves out the country of origin from the third altogether.)*

We write for our readers. Readers like to see equal proportion in our word choice and sentence construction. Balance, like cadence helps readers follow along comfortably, enjoying the writer's work and at the same time comprehending the intended message. However, like a washing machine that thunks and groans when the clothes become unbalanced, unequal or non-parallel sentences disturb readers, take them out of the world you have created, and make them aware of errors or problems.

Readers crave symmetry in writing, as do listeners, which is why songwriters include a chorus in each piece they write. The chorus grounds or balances the song and creates a recognizable pattern. Good writers understand how symmetry in their work also functions as a chorus. *The Thomson Handbook* quotes one of the most famous uses of parallelism, Abraham Lincoln's "Gettysburg Address" in which he states,

> " . . . and that this government **of the people, by the people, for the people** shall not perish from this earth."

We have to assume Lincoln knew how similar speeches are to songs and that the chorus is the catchy part of a song, the part we learn first and thus remember most, so he deliberately created a memorable parallel sentence. Imagine that sentence without the "chorus":

> " . . . and that this government **of the people** shall not perish from this earth."

Nice, but is it memorable enough to quote 143 years later?

To keep your readers immersed in your writing, you must write parallel, imagining your sentences as little scales or see-saws, and you must strive to stay even.

Parallel Items in a Series

On Friday Fay decided to **change** her hair style, **buy** a new outfit, and **go** out to dinner. *(All verbs are present tense and lead off each element in the series.)*

Penguins **are black and white birds, are shaped like missiles,** and **are warm blooded.**

In choosing an apartment, Stuart knew he wanted one with **a dishwasher, a view of the woods,** and **a balcony.**

Parallel Items in Pairs

Whereas the **parallel items in a series** mostly include lists of three or more items, **parallelism with paired items** occurs when an author discusses two equal or matching words, phrases, or clauses.

When Joey left for college his parents were **sad** but **excited** at the same time. *(two competing emotions)*

The movie focused on **global warming** and **world hunger.** *(both issues receiving the same attention)*

Correlative conjunctions, which we discussed in Chapter 9, also indicate parallel pairs.

Either you are **with us** *or* **against us.** (Either/or *denotes there is nothing more than these two equivalent choices.*)

After reading the menu carefully, Amanda decided she wanted *both* **a salad** *and* **a pizza** for her lunch. *(Neither subordinates the other.)*

Parallelism in Lists and Outlines

Whether for yourself (an informal outline) or for an assignment (a formal outline), when making lists always keep items in parallel structure.

- Keep numerology consistent (I, II, III or 1, 2, 3 but not I, 2, III).
- Write either in complete sentences or in explicit words or phrases.
- Keep capitalization consistent.
- Be consistent in writing style in each level if using sub-numbering or lettering.

An outline for a paper analyzing the recent popularity of coffee among college students:

I. Introduction
    A. How coffee has become a social outlet and a necessity to studying
    B. Brief data supporting rising trend in consumption
    C. Thesis
II. Body
    A. Reports from Coffee Lovers, Inc.
    B. Interviews from students on campus

C. My analysis of the data

D. My conclusions

III. Conclusion

    A. People use coffee as an excuse for socializing

    B. People use coffee as a stimulant to stay awake for class and studying

    C. Studies show coffee helps circulation and other health benefits

Parallelism in Headings

Writers utilize headings in lab reports, proposals, evaluations, and other scholarly papers. Like the wording in a sentence, headings also must be parallel in nature to create balance and ease of reading.

Technology Toolbox

Inserting Headings into Your Writing

Headings can help you keep your writing organized and the content of your papers more obvious to your readers. Headings are also very important to Web pages because studies show readers scan for important information. Unlike a printed document where readers may flip through many pages to find headings, many Web pages contain lots of information on one screen. To make the heading stand out, either **bold** or <u>underline</u> the text. Whichever style you choose, be consistent throughout. Since space is at a premium, parallel Web headings also often act as direct links, so headings literally transport your readers from place to place. Mismatched or non-parallel headings will cause your readers to leave your site.

Revising Faulty Parallelism

A faulty sentence occurs when the author fails to recognize the pattern or balance between equal ideas in the sentence. Revising the wording usually fixes the error.

Faulty:

For my Western Civilization paper, I am either going to cover women's roles in the Revolutionary War or the Napoleonic Wars. *(faulty because the reader expects the second element to also pertain to women's roles)*

Revised:

For my Western Civilization paper, I am either going to cover women's roles in the Revolutionary War or <u>women's roles in the Napoleonic wars</u>.

Faulty:

The speaker discussed the effects of genocide on African countries, their governments are filled with corrupt officials, the problems due to poverty, and the issues surrounding the AIDS epidemic. *(The second element in the series is not parallel in structure with the others.)*

Revised:

The speaker discussed the effects of genocide on African countries, <u>the issues surrounding corruption of government officials</u>, the problems due to poverty, and the issues surrounding the AIDS epidemic.

Faulty

3 Reasons to major in Biology

1. It's my favorite subject
2. horticulture
3. Jobs and travel

Revised

3 Reasons to Major in Biology

1. It's my favorite subject
2. I love horticulture
3. There are job and travel opportunities

Level 1

Name_____ **Date**_____

DIRECTIONS Rewrite the following sentences to make parallel structures out of the listed items. When you revise the sentence, underline the parallel items.

SAMPLE

Jane reads mystery novels because she likes the challenge of solving the case and most of them are suspenseful.

Jane reads mystery novels because she likes _the challenge_ of solving the case and _the suspense._

1. The hard-boiled private eye novels, the cultured sleuth series, and novels with innocent little old lady detectives are Jane's favorites.

   _____

   _____

2. Her passion for the mysteries began when she took an English course where she learned the plot strategies, how to create believable characters, and honesty.

   _____

   _____

3. A good detective usually follows the same pattern. He or she sees the world as cruel. The streets are mean. Also the detective has some kind of resentment for authority.

   _____

   _____

4. Edgar Allen Poe is credited with originating the mystery genre with stories like "The Murders at Rue Morgue," "The Purloined Letter," "The Mystery of Marie Roget," and other stories like "The Gold-Bug," and "The Tell-Tale Heart."

   _____

   _____

5. Over 2 billion Agatha Christie books have been sold to fans who love her quirky characters, quaint villages, the realism of her writing, and her amusing detectives, particularly Hercule Poiroit and Miss Jane Marple.

_____

_____

Level 1

Name_____ **Date**_____

DIRECTIONS Revise the non-parallel element(s) so the sentences are parallel in structure.

SAMPLE

On vacation Joseph likes reading, sunbathing, and going for bike rides.

_On vacation Joseph likes reading, sunbathing, and biking._____

_____

1. Shanna and Joseph went to Aruba to enjoy the beaches, looking for seashells to add to their collection, and to go snorkeling.

_____

_____

2. The couple stayed at a resort where they expected excellent service and they wanted free coupons to local attractions.

_____

_____

3. On the snorkel boat the instructor explained that they should rinse their masks before putting them on, that they should pick a buddy and stay with that person, and to keep an eye on the boat.

_____

_____

4. At night Shanna and Joseph like to try the local restaurants and they also eat in the hotel dining room.

_____

_____

5. Shanna enjoys sunbathing at the beach more than when she goes snorkeling.

   _____

   _____

6. Aruba is noted for its wild iguanas, beautiful beaches, exquisite water, and that tourists are welcome.

   _____

   _____

Level 1

Name_____ **Date**_____

DIRECTIONS Underline the parallel item(s) and then rewrite the following to add the missing item(s) in the pair, the list, or the heading to create a parallel structure.

SAMPLE

I am neither sad nor _____ that the movie ended the way it did.

I am neither sad nor disappointed that the movie ended the way it did.

1. Do you want to get Mexican food for dinner or _____?

2. We should either study for our midterm tonight or _____.

3. Sometimes I think cell phones are important but other times _____

_____.

4. When Steve goes to the gym he enjoys lifting weights and _____.

5. Whether the weather is sunny or _____ Steve makes sure he goes to the gym five days a week.

6. Reasons to Exercise:
   I. Improves cardiovascular health
      A. Heart is a muscle that needs exertion
      B. Increased heart rate promotes blood flow

Level 2

Name_____ **Date**_____

DIRECTIONS Revise the following sentences so they are parallel in structure.

SAMPLE

When they were in Boston, Pam and Kathy saw the Red Sox play at Fenway Park, walked around the old neighborhood, and a bus ride to Faneuil Hall was in order.

When they were in Boston, Pam and Kathy saw the Red Sox play at Fenway

Park, walked around their old neighborhood, and took a bus to Faneuil Hall.

1. In Fenway Park fans can sit in "The Belly," behind "Pesky's Pole," "near "Duffy's Cliff," and then there is the "Lone Red Seat" in the right field bleachers.

_____

_____

2. The stadium's famous "Green Monster" is a screen that protects the street behind the park from foul balls because it is 37 feet high, 230 feet long, 22 feet deep, and weighs 30,000 pounds of iron.

_____

_____

3. Faneuil Hall has been a thriving marketplace and people use it as a meeting hall.

_____

_____

4. Pam and Kathy enjoyed taking the Freedom Trail almost as much as when they went to Fenway Park.

_____

_____

5. Tourists and locals in Boston appreciate the rich history and they also like the fresh seafood choices.

_____

_____

6. Beacon Hill, South Boston, Mission Hill, and Mattapan are neighborhoods in Boston. Dorchester and Hyde Park are too.

_____

_____

7. The Strand Youth Theater Project is an after school program that teaches kids basic acting skills, monologue work, and group performance work is also concentrated on.

_____

_____

8. Boston is known for its place in history, its culture and art, and there is the largest Citgo sign in New England in Kenmore Square.

_____

_____

9. The Citgo sign was constructed of five miles of neon tubing, and is 60 feet by 60 feet. It is the size of an Olympic size pool.

_____

_____

Writing Clearly, Cleanly, and Concisely

The Thomson Handbook, **Chapter 36**

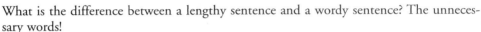

What is the difference between a lengthy sentence and a wordy sentence? The unnecessary words!

It is no coincidence that writers develop more confidence in expressing their ideas as they grow older and acquire more sophisticated vocabularies. However, along with a greater range of expression come certain bad writing habits, namely writing that is blown out of proportion by wordiness, exaggerated sentences, and unnecessary verbiage.

Wordiness

There are many reasons why we bulk up our sentences. For one, long, protracted sentences were all the rage in 19th century writing, so we have a history of this way of writing. An author of the period might pen:

> "Oh dear reader, to be desirous of the company of that man called Wentworth shall certainly fill me with dread and regret."

Whereas today's author would write:

> "I cannot stand Wentworth."

Today's authors are exposed to many regularly used phrases when shorter, more concise verbiage works better.

Wordy:
<u>In light of the fact that</u> the electricity went out in my house, I <u>was regrettably unable to</u> complete my homework.

Revised:
Because of a power failure, I could not complete my homework. *(None of the wording from the previous sentence is needed for the reader to understand the meaning.)*

Wordy:
<u>In an effort to</u> calm his nerves, Steven paced backstage before the show started.

Revised:
Steven paced backstage to calm his nerves before the show started. *(Rewording the sentence to place* Steven *as the subject reduces the need for extra explanation.)*

Wordy:
I am <u>actually</u> a fan of the theater, though my least favorite genre <u>would have to be that of the musical.</u>

Revised:

I am a theater fan, though the musical is my least favorite genre. *(Although actually is an often used expression to denote emphasis, it is unnecessary. For emphasis, substitute a stronger word.)*

Wordy:

<u>It seems to be a fact</u> that any play involving Andrew Lloyd Weber is bound to be a success.

Revised:

Andrew Lloyd Weber's plays all seem successful.

Unnecessary Use of Self

Yet another problem of unnecessary verbiage involves inserting oneself in the writing.

Wordy:

<u>It seems to me</u> Morrison's use of the school primer in *The Bluest Eye* symbolizes the standard of whiteness all Americans felt they must mimic.

Revised:

In *The Bluest Eye* Morrison uses the school primer to symbolize the standard of whiteness all Americans felt they must mimic.

Wordy:

Morrison's debut novel, <u>in my opinion,</u> never achieved its due with the critics.

Revised:

Morrison's debut novel never achieved its due with the critics.

Clichés

Writers who are unsure of themselves often cheapen their prose by filling sentences with empty phrases like clichés.

Wordy:

<u>Back in the day</u> we thought going to the mall was cool.

Revised:

When we were younger we thought going to the mall was cool.

Wordy:

<u>In today's society</u> certain topics are too controversial to discuss in public.

Revised:

Currently, certain topics are too controversial for public discussion.

Unnecessary Repetition

Filler words are usually the result of needless repetition of an idea or concept that can appear in just one sentence or become carried over into adjoining sentences.

Wordy:

Bob knew Janie wanted to paint the bathroom. He took her to the paint store to pick out the paint and then painted the bathroom.

Revised:

Since Bob knew Janie wanted the bathroom repainted, he took her to the paint store and then repainted the bathroom that day. *(combining sentences reduces redundancy)*

Wordy:

The <u>ancient, decrepit</u> door swung open with rusty groan.

Revised:

The decrepit door swung open with a rusty groan. (Ancient *and* decrepit *repeat the same idea.*)

Wordy:

I take a multivitamin <u>each and every day</u>.

Revised:

I take a multivitamin every day. (Every day *expresses the same concept.*)

Wordy:

Musicians Sheryl Crow and Melissa Etheridge have both been in the news. Crow and Etheridge made the news because of their battles with breast cancer.

Revised:

Musicians Sheryl Crow and Melissa Etheridge have been in the news regarding their respective battles with breast cancer.

Strategies to Eliminate Wordiness and Repetition

- Read your drafts for repetition.

Find and Replace

Use the "Find" function under "Edit" to locate a word you might have overused, like *I* or the subject of your paper. You may be astounded when you read how many times you used the word! You can then select "Replace" to easily change or correct some instances of the overused word. Holding down the "Ctrl" and "F" keys at the same time will also bring up the Find function.

- Learn to avoid multiple sentences and repetitious terms. Use the thesaurus to help you find alternatives and sprinkle in pronouns when possible.

Wordy:

After graduation Danielle applied for a position as a writer with *National Geographic*. Danielle was president of the Ecology Club and figured her experience would help. Danielle also majored in English and minored in Biology, so she thought her writing experience would be a positive in the hiring.

Revised:

After graduation, Danielle applied her experience as an English major and Biology minor to submit an application for a position with *National Geographic*.

- Combine sentences by appositives.

  An appositive is a noun or a noun phrase used as an adjective to rename a noun or pronoun.

Wordy:

Bobby Wharton is a local businessman. He co-owns The Crab Shack and Schooners.

Revised:

Bobby Wharton, <u>a local businessman,</u> co-owns The Crab Shack and Schooners.

■ Combine sentences with a compound.

As we discussed in Chapter 9, a compound sentence joins shorter sentences with a **coordinating conjunction** or **correlative conjunction.**

Wordy:

Melanie is Bobby's wife. Melanie has a decorating business and raises their three children.

Revised:

Bobby's wife Melanie raises their three children <u>and</u> owns a decorating business.

■ Reduce wordiness with complex sentences.

Also in Chapter 9 we discussed how to apply a variety of skills to make complex sentences, including using **subordination, transitions, correlative conjunctions, semicolons, and colons.**

Wordy:

Bridget enjoys tinkering with her *Facebook* profile. *Facebook* is an online social network. You have to be a member to see *Facebook* profiles.

Revised:

Bridget enjoys tinkering with her profile on *Facebook,* the online, members only, social network.

Wordy:

Kate took a Web writing course in order to learn how to write on the Internet. Writing on the Internet is quite different from print writing she discovered.

Revised:

Kate took a Web writing course and discovered writing on the Internet is quite different from print.

Level 1

Name_____ **Date**_____

DIRECTIONS Draw a line through all evidence of wordy prose you find in the following sentences. Then rewrite the sentence for clarity.

SAMPLE

~~As it was in the beginning of time~~ coffee has ~~actually~~ always been a popular beverage.

People have been drinking coffee for thousands of years.

1. Though not yet conclusively proven, recent studies suggest coffee consumption does not in fact increase the risk of heart attack.

   _____

   _____

2. Regarding other health benefits, coffee has been discovered to contain an abundant and rich source of antioxidants. Americans get their antioxidants from coffee more than any other possible food source.

   _____

   _____

3. Cyclists and runners can rejoice aloud to know that in this day and age health professionals believe drinking coffee increases stamina and decreases evidence of leg pain and fatigue.

   _____

   _____

4. In order to completely understand the complex situation of caffeine and its attendant effects on the human body, the harmful effects must also be taken into consideration.

   _____

   _____

5. In all the studies showcasing the positive and supportive sides of coffee, it seems worthy to note that studies demonstrating the caffeine contained in coffee restricts an individual's blood vessels.

_____

_____

6. Several medical studies suggest a link between caffeine intake and breast cancer, for example, though to be in agreement with that fact might be difficult with numerous other studies suggesting no actual or real evidence exists to support such findings.

_____

_____

7. In yet another study scientists have determined that coffee may counteract and circumvent the poisonous and detrimental effects alcohol consumption has on the liver, most specifically cirrhosis.

_____

_____

8. To be specific, the liver study pertains to the heavy alcoholic whose liver has been permanently damaged by extensive alcohol consumption, not the casual, occasional drinker who only drinks every now and again.

_____

_____

9. Naturally, the best way to avoid dangerously harmful diseases like cirrhosis of the liver is to abstain totally from heavily drinking alcohol, it should be said.

_____

_____

10. In view of the fact that virtually most or all scientific studies compiled by experts confirm that moderation is the key to the coffee consumption situation, one must conclude that one or two coffee beverages per day would not unduly stress the body.

_____

_____

Level 1

Name_____ Date_____

DIRECTIONS Draw a line through all clichés you find in the following sentences. Then rewrite the sentence for clarity. In many cases you must interpret the author's meaning.

SAMPLE

My grandmother always said, "~~Idle hands are the devil's workshop,~~" when she saw me goofing off.

_My grandmother believed in staying busy._____

1. The Enron scandal and subsequent trials prove that absolute power corrupts absolutely.

   _____

   _____

2. The top officials in the company pretended to be honest as the day is long when in fact they were stealing money from employees and making suspicious business deals.

   _____

   _____

3. As luck would have it, the big brass got caught, proving every dog has his day.

   _____

   _____

4. Even though in this country people are guilty until proven innocent, Kenneth Lay and Jeffery Schilling were behind the 8 ball in most people's eyes.

   _____

   _____

5. When the two were explaining the business at hand, they tried to confuse the facts with a barrage of evidence.

   _____

   _____

6. Many Enron employees who lost their pensions were thrilled with the news that Lay and Schilling had been busted, but they doubted the court's ability to get their man.

_____

_____

Level 1

Name_____ **Date**_____

DIRECTIONS Draw a line through all clichés and personal references you believe unnecessary to the sentence's meaning in the following sentences. Then rewrite the sentence for clarity. In many cases you must interpret the author's meaning.

SAMPLE

Buying a car, so I discovered, is about ~~as easy as chewing nails and spitting tacks.~~

Buying a car was the most difficult experience ever.

1. As I arrived at the dealership I noticed the sales staff circling around like a pack of hungry dogs waiting for their victim.

   _____

   _____

2. Not to be deterred, I was ready for a battle due to the fact that I had done ample research and was ready to negotiate.

   _____

   _____

3. Having settled for the hybrid Civic, the best car for the fuel crisis in this day and age, I began choosing color, options, and other fun choices.

   _____

   _____

4. Prior to settling on the final price, the person I was dealing with from the car company suggested I purchase the protection package with reference to rust under the car, stains on the seats, and problems with the paint.

   _____

   _____

5. It seems to me that in the event of a problem with paint, rust, or the seats I could handle the problem myself, so I opted out of the protection plan. Besides, it costs too much.

_____

_____

6. I recommend to anyone out there to arm yourself to the teeth before you negotiate for a car, used or new. I know that in order to make money, dealerships, like any other business, must be tough.

_____

_____

Level 1

Name_____ **Date**_____

DIRECTIONS Rewrite each of the following wordy sentences by reducing repetition. You may move elements around to rank the main and the subordinate ideas.

SAMPLE

American Sign Language (ASL) is a language used by the deaf community in America and Canada. This language has a complex grammar component.

The preferred communication method for most deaf Americans and Canadians is the American Sign Language (ASL), which has a complex grammar component.

1. ASL has been referred to as a "gestural" language. This means ASL is done completely by hand movement.

   _____

   _____

2. ASL is gestural. Also, ASL uses facial expressions like lip movements and eyebrow movements. ASL also uses the space immediately around the signer that is used to describe people or places not in the room or space.

   _____

   _____

3. Contrary to popular belief, ASL is not universal. ASL is not universal because it is based on English. Japanese deaf use JSL and French use FSL. These are just a couple of examples of international signing.

   _____

   _____

4. ASL is difficult for deaf-impaired. The deaf-impaired are the hearing. Many find it difficult to understand the rules for creating words and rules for handshapes. The ASL grammar rules are hard to learn too.

   _____

   _____

5. The best way to learn ASL is to learn from a hearing impaired person. Another good way to learn is to read the journals and texts about ASL.

_____

_____

Level 2

Name_____ **Date**_____

DIRECTIONS Rewrite each of the following wordy sentences by reducing repetition. You may move elements around to rank the main and the subordinate ideas.

Elena decided to take a pottery class. Due to the fact that she was a sophomore, she felt that the time was right and it was now or never. She was excited to begin the class. On the first day of the class the teacher let them make a coil pot. A coil pot is long rolls of clay. The long rolls of clay are then wound around on top of each other. Eventually a coil pot is built. In the second week the students began wedging clay. Wedging clay is a process of folding it over and over to get the air bubbles out. Why do you need to get the air bubbles out? An air bubble will explode in the kiln when the pot is cooking. If there is an air bubble and it explodes, the pot is destroyed. The pot could also destroy other pots nearby. Elena learned clay wedging is good for arm strength on account of each clay wedge must be wedged 100 times for good measure. Once she began learning how to make pots on the wheel, Elena was thrilled. She kept thinking about holiday and birthday presents. She also thought she could save money by giving her pots and mugs out as presents. People love handmade pottery. At art shows handmade pottery is expensive. So are presents so Elena figured everyone was a winner in this strategy.

_____

_____

_____

_____

_____

_____

_____

_____

_____

_____

Word Choices to Enhance Your Writing

The Thomson Handbook, Chapter 38

Many times as writers we know *what* we want to convey but struggle with *how* to say it, the process of picking which words best express our thoughts.

   Part of the conundrum is understanding how many lexicons (sets of words) we consciously and unconsciously know and use, and which circumstance is right for which vocabulary. Basically, we can divide our speaking and writing patterns into two styles:

- Public discourse: communication we wish for others to receive
- Private discourse: communication that is only for ourselves

Then, we have to break these two divisions down further to understand appropriate language choice.

Public Discourse

Public discourse includes both formal and informal writing.

Formal writing uses Standard Written English (see *The Thomson Handbook,* p. 771) for papers and assignments, letters to superiors or requesting jobs, memos, and other writing for record keeping purposes. Writers maintain distance by refraining from using the *I* and *you* personal pronouns.

> In the "Aeolus" episode of *Ulysses, Freeman's Journal* editor Myles Crawford lays a hand on the shoulder of Stephen Dedalus and tells the young man, "I want you to write something for me. Something with a bite in it. You can do it. I see it in your face. . . . Put us all into it, damn its soul" (111). Critics have long identified *Ulysses* as that piece of writing that self-consciously executes the newspaper editor's demand, but early Joyce critics such as biographer Richard Ellmann, it is now charged, left the novel toothless rather than biting, privileging its modernist aesthetic and supposed universal humanism over its specific, political concerns. These approaches either "defang[ed]" Joyce's purported nationalism as Vincent Cheng claims in *Joyce, Race, and Empire* (2), or they just flat-out ignored it, attributing both to Joyce and to his work what Emer Nolan has referred to as a "benign multiculturalism" (3). (Tracey Teets Schwarze, "History's Echo")

Informal writing may be as relaxed as a note to your roommate, friend, or a family member, or something not quite as formal as Standard Written English but that will be read and maybe evaluated, such as a lab report, an interview, some assignments, homework, and even a blog, or email. Personal references using *I* and *you* are commonplace.

> Fri, 09/16/2005 - 14:48
>
> A friend I were just wondering about this the other day in response to <u>Water crisis looms as Himalayan glaciers melt.</u> Is there anything we can do to stop global warming? Probably not according to a recent study of Arctic ice melting discussed in <u>Global warming 'past the point of</u>

no return'. It looks like it's time to start developing technologies to assist in coping with the drastic climatic changes we will see over the next 50 to 100 years. (cyberdash's blog)

Private Discourse

Private discourse includes journal and diary entries that are not published, reminder notes to oneself, day planner or calendar entries.

Colloquialisms

A type of informal discourse that should never appear in formal writing, colloquial language is what most people use to communicate in "everyday speech." Not to be confused with **slang** or **regional dialogue,** a colloquial writer or speaker uses contractions, short-cut phrases, and other condensed versions of words or terms.

> We can't wait to see you again, so hurry up and get on the road.

> Give us a phone call when you get close to the county line and we'll start looking for you.

We usually understand when to switch gears out of our **informal** or **colloquial** expressions.

> "Hey Mom, what's up? How about dropping me $20?"

We know when to use more **formal** expressions.

> "Dear Mom, unfortunately, I have run out of money. Would you please mail me a check for $20?"

Slang

Slang has no place in college writing, but it is very important because it often defines a peer group or cultural identity, from cliques in high school to specialized professionals at NASA. Slang also seems to separate people into age groups, because what is popular and commonplace among a group of college freshmen may not be appealing or familiar to their professors.

Slang by the Decade:	Term	Definition
1920s:	bimbo	tough guy
	dogs	a person's feet
	moll	a gangster's girlfriend
1950s:	cruisin' for a bruisin'	looking for a fight
	frosted	angry
	hottie	fast car
1990s:	da bomb	something excellent
	dogpack	circle of friends
	peaceout	goodbye
2000s:	sweet	excellent, wonderful
	fall out	go to sleep
	hottie	attractive person
	punk	embarrass or play a joke

Though some slang terms make it into commonly used language, most slip out of use rather quickly.

Regionalisms

Many phrases or expressions are **idiomatic,** that is they originate and are practiced by a particular geographic area in the country, which means these phrases may not carry over to other geographic regions.

In the South, a dark-colored carbonated beverage is typically called a *coke,* whereas in the North the same drink is called a *soda,* and in the Midwest, a *pop.*

In Great Britain a *yank* is an American, but in America a *yank* is short for *Yankee,* presumably a person from the North.

Remember, the level of formality depends upon the audience and the purpose. When in doubt, err on the formal side. College writers should not employ colloquialisms, regional dialect, or slang in their work. Writing informally should be at the professor's consent, especially for a paper or graded assignment.

Technology Toolbox

The Spelling and Grammar Advanced Functions

Your word processor's Spelling and Grammar function gives you the choice of checking your documents for "grammar only" or for "grammar and style." If you want to check for problems like slang, jargon, and contractions, go to your toolbox, find the spelling and grammar option, choose "Options" and pick "Grammar and Style." You can also decide which issues you want the program to look for under "Settings."

As always, remember that this program is not completely accurate, but it gives you a good starting point.

Simple and Safe to Elegant and Sophisticated Vocabularies

Most students begin their college careers taking few chances, preferring instead to stick with strategies that worked well in the past and got them into college. This system will work for a short while, but as you become involved in the discourse (language) communities of the university, both your expectations and those of your professors will be for your writing to grow in sophistication.

One sure way to raise your confidence and probably also your grades is to work on gradually and carefully expanding your vocabulary. Often this process is natural because you pick up new words from your readings, from class discussions, and from your peers. However, these sources do not provide enough resources, which is where these two strategies will help raise your vocabulary from the simple and safe to the elegant and sophisticated.

- Invest in a good thesaurus. Almost any bookstore sells paperback and hardback thesauruses. Your word processor also has a limited thesaurus located in the Tools option, and you can find an online thesaurus at http://www.dictionary.com

  The point of a thesaurus is to provide *subtle* help to assist you as you move from simple and safe to elegant and sophisticated. You should not attempt to find alternatives for every word, nor should you use words you cannot understand.

  Remember the episode of *Friends* when Joey convinces Chandler and Monica he can write a good letter of recommendation for the adoption agency they are using? When Joey worries to Ross that he does not sound "smart enough" Ross explains how a thesaurus would help. Joey writes his letter and proudly gives it to Monica and Chandler:

Monica: It doesn't make any sense.

Joey: Of course it does. It's smart! I used a thesaurus!

Chandler: On every word?

Joey: Yep.

Monica: All right, what was this sentence, originally?

Joey: Oh. "They're warm, nice people with big hearts."

Chandler: And that became, "They're humid, pre-possessing homo sapiens with full-sized aortic pumps?"

Obviously exercising moderation and understanding his audience and purpose would have helped Joey, but he became too immersed in vocabulary options.

- Create a personal thesaurus of words you like to use in your writing but might not always remember. You can separate this list by subject matter so all your humanities options are apart from your sciences vocabulary, or you can list by word type, like verbs and phrases.

- Instead of trying to elaborate and expand your entire vocabulary at once, begin with verbs, because a sentence containing a strong verb instead of a weak one demonstrates strength and authority.

Weak
Diane **is** majoring in Chemistry.
Shane is a good writer.
I **have been** to Germany recently.
Alicia **was pleased** with her grade.

Strong
Diane **chose** to major in Chemistry.
Shane **writes** well.
I recently **traveled** to Germany.
Alicia **feels good** about her grade.

Level 1

Name_____ **Date**_____

DIRECTIONS The following response was submitted as an *informal journal writing assignment.* Rewrite the paragraph so that it is appropriate for a *formal writing assignment.*

SAMPLE

I do not want to sacrifice my style to the point where I no longer recognize my voice merely so that my Web site will be more accessible to the average individual.

Web authors should not sacrifice writing style to appeal to the average Internet audience member.

Melanie Beahm
Journal Response to Homework

After reading an article detailing the ways in which several companies prevent their users from conveniently and rapidly accessing information, I expected to be angry at such organizations for their carelessness; instead, I found myself more frustrated with society and the millions of people who navigate the Internet. I understand that individuals want to complete tasks quickly, but how much effort is really necessary to read information thoroughly or to wait a few seconds or minutes for a page to reload? Maybe I do not visit enough Web sites, or perhaps the Internet has improved in recent years, because I have never encountered the extent of the troubles that the article we read for homework mentions.

_____

_____

_____

_____

_____

_____

_____

_____

_____

_____

Level 1

Name_____ **Date**_____

DIRECTIONS The following is an excerpt from a private journal. Revise all slang, colloquial expressions, and use of regional dialect to be appropriate for a formal writing assignment.

SAMPLE

Cait got a job and she is making mad money.

*Cait makes good money at her new job.*_____

    If I was a musical instrument I would be an electric guitar, the baddest of the bad, because a player would hold me lovingly and play me until the cows come home. The electric guitar can be an angry, loud, screaming freakshow showing its listeners that something fierce is trying to escape. It can also twang the most melodic notes to soothe the savage beast from within.

    Diversity makes this instrument the rock star of the music world, and diversity expresses my personality best. The people who play electric guitars represent that diversity. Just think, a righteous dude like B. B. King has his beloved guitar, Lucille, and a whack like Angus Young of AC/DC struts around in a schoolboy uniform playing the heck outta his guitar, and these dudes are in the same category!

_____

_____

_____

_____

_____

_____

_____

_____

_____

_____

_____

_____

_____

Level 1

Name_____ Date_____

DIRECTIONS Each of the following sentences is written in a "safe" style that does not use strong verbs. Using a thesaurus, revise each sentence to replace the weak verb with a strong verb. To get more information about this exercise's subject matter go to: http://nationalzoo.si.edu/default.cfm

SAMPLE

The National Zoo in Washington D.C. is one of the finest in the nation.

One of the finest in the nation, the National Zoo in Washington D.C.

contains many endangered species and animals from all over the world.

(The revised version explains why the zoo is so acclaimed.)

1. The first cheetahs born in the zoo have been moved to different zoos as part of a cheetah conservation project.

_____

_____

2. On July 9, 2006, Giant Panda cub Tian Shan had his first birthday.

_____

_____

3. The zoo's Web site has etiquette instructions for people who want to get to know the apes.

_____

_____

4. The ferret exhibit is next to the prairie dog exhibit, and the ferret is the natural enemy of the prairie dog!

_____

_____

5. There is an "octopus cam" on the zoo's Web site which is good for people at home.

_____

_____

6. There are a lot of opportunities to learn about conservation at the zoo and on their Web site.

_____

_____

Level 1

Name_____ **Date**_____

DIRECTIONS Each of the following sentences needs revision to take it out of the safe zone and correct errors in colloquialism, slang, and regionalism. Using a thesaurus, rewrite each sentence to replace weak or unimaginative wording.

SAMPLE

Photojournalism **is** about using photos to **tell** stories.

Photojournalists employ photography to document life.

1. Most professional photographers use digital cameras instead of 35 mm ones.

_____

_____

2. Digital cameras give the photographer more freedom to shoot and reshoot. They are also cheaper since the person can delete instead of get pictures they don't want.

_____

_____

3. Digital pictures are easy to fix using various computer software programs.

_____

_____

4. Many people don't like posed pictures, and very few think posed shots are part of photojournalism.

_____

_____

5. When you see a color picture in the paper that looks fuzzy, it is called "out of register."

_____

_____

6. Out of register photos are harder to print because the printer uses 4 kinds of color ink. Printers for big newspapers can be the size of a two-story house, so alignment problems are common.

_____

_____

7. Most professional photographers think black and white pictures are the best. Most amateur photographers like color pictures.

_____

_____

8. Professional photographers have it difficult, especially those on assignment in harsh conditions like third-world countries, wars, and in the jungle.

_____

_____

9. Light and camera angle are the difference between a great photo and an average one.

_____

_____

10. You need your own camera to sign up for the Photojournalism course.

_____

_____

11. It has been said that a picture is worth a thousand words. If that is so, why don't newspapers print more pictures?

_____

_____

Level 2

Name_____ **Date**_____

DIRECTIONS The following sentences from an essay need revision to take them out of the safe zone and correct errors in colloquialism, slang, and regionalism. Using a thesaurus, rewrite each sentence to replace weak or unimaginative wording. To get more information about this exercise's subject you may want to do a Web search for "rock climbing." If so, write the url you used here:

SAMPLE

Rock climbing is a sport where people use very little equipment to scale or climb steep hills or mountains.

Athletes called rock climbers scale steep hills and mountains using their hands, feet, and ropes.

1. The sport has become very popular in the last fifteen years. More people want to climb.

_____

_____

2. Climbers can use indoor facilities or go to extremes, depending on their level of interest.

_____

_____

3. Most free climbers believe that equipment is for safety only. They believe climbers are to use their hands, feet, and skills.

_____

_____

4. The basic equipment: shoes with hard rubber bottoms, rope, carabiners, webbing, harnesses, and the belayer.

_____

_____

5. The beyaler is a person who is lower than the climber or higher if he or she is the lead belayer. The belayer has a rope attached to an anchor and to the climber. The belayer stops the climber from falling during an accident.

_____

_____

6. Once someone has gotten to the top, he or she can get down by walking, rappelling, or the belayer can lower the person.

_____

_____

7. The best way to get going is to practice on smaller rock formations. Climbers need strong hands, strong arms, strong backs, strong legs, and strong feet. Weight training is not necessary but is a good idea to build strength. Rock climbing is a good sport for men and women.

_____

_____

8. After the climber has trained and read up on the sport, he or she is ready to begin. A good place to start is through a group. You can find other rock climbers online or at a local outdoors sporting shop.

_____

_____

9. During bad weather the rock gym is a good place to practice and stay in shape. Many rock climbing gyms offer lessons.

_____

_____

Writing Solid Paragraphs

The Thomson Handbook, **Chapter 5**

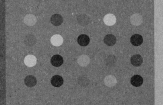

By learning the parts of speech and how they function cohesively, which word choice works best for your purposes, and how to enhance your vocabulary, you have assembled all the workings of a paragraph, a paper, a Web site, or any written project you undertake.

Now you can begin making everything fit appropriately. A **paragraph** is composed of connected or complementary sentences. Paragraphs can stand alone, but they are usually part of a larger piece of writing consisting of multiple paragraphs.

Learning how to properly identify the parts of a paragraph and replicate them in your own paragraphs is the biggest step in the writing process.

Paragraph FAQs

- What is a paragraph?

  A paragraph is a group of sentences clustered into a single grammatical unit because they pertain to a single idea or thought. Paragraphs can either stand alone or be part of a larger piece of writing.

- What should I include in a paragraph?

  No matter how long or short, a paragraph must contain a **topic sentence, supporting material, transitions,** and a **concluding sentence,** unless it contains dialogue (see below).

  The topic sentence describes the paragraph's **main idea.** Think of the topic sentence as the **thesis** for the paragraph. Typically, the **topic sentence** begins the paragraph so readers can immediately understand the author's point, but some writers place it at the end of the paragraph or somewhere in the middle. A few sophisticated writers are able to imply the central idea of the paragraph and not create a specific topic sentence.

  The **supporting material** consists of the evidence to prove or demonstrate the point of the topic sentence. If your topic sentence is: "There should be no curfews in the dorms on weekends," then the supporting material explains to your readers why you feel this way.

  Transitions are words or phrases that gently guide your readers from point to point. If you list three reasons why the curfew should be suspended in the dorms on weekends, your transitions might include: **The first reason** the curfew should be suspended. . . **Next**. . . **Finally**. . .

  Always end a paragraph with a **concluding sentence** to wrap up or finish the issue and transition into the next point.

Example

Topic sentence:

On this campus there should be no curfews in the dorms on weekends because residents want to be treated like adults with trust; fewer residents are on campus on weekends; and people tend to stay up later and sleep in on the weekend.

Supporting material with transitions:

- According to random surveys conducted in York River East and West, students resent continually having to prove they are as responsible during the weekend as they are during the week.

- **Also,** an article in the school newspaper revealed that about 6% of residents go home or visit friends during the weekend.

- **Additionally,** a survey conducted in James River East and West revealed that even though many residents stay up late during the week, significantly more students stay up late and sleep in on the weekend.

Concluding sentence:

Essentially, the overwhelming evidence of student opinion should suffice in overturning the weekend curfew in the resident halls.

Putting the Pieces Together

The information above pieced into traditional paragraph form would look like this:

On this campus there should be no curfews in the dorms on weekends because residents want to be treated like adults with trust, fewer residents are on campus on weekends, and people tend to stay up later and sleep in on the weekend. According to random surveys conducted in York River East and West, students resent continually having to prove they are as responsible during the weekend as they are during the week. Also, an article in the school newspaper revealed that about 6% of residents go home or visit friends during the weekend. Additionally, a survey conducted in James River East and West revealed that even though many residents stay up late during the week, significantly more students stay up late and sleep in on the weekend. Essentially, the overwhelming evidence of student opinion should suffice in overturning the weekend curfew in the residence halls.

- What should I not include in a paragraph?

The topic sentence dictates what should be included in a paragraph. If your topic sentence is:

"The male lion's physical prowess is impressive," you may not discuss anything in your paragraph that does not pertain to physical attributes of a male lion.

When you want to introduce new material, simply start a new paragraph.

If you write about a process where you explain step-by-step instructions, begin a new paragraph for each stage.

If you are writing a dialogue, each speaker begins a new paragraph.

In formal papers, the introductory paragraph and the concluding paragraph are separate from the rest of the work.

- I learned the "Five Paragraph Rule." Does that apply to college writing?

Only by coincidence would the Five Paragraph Rule apply to writing you do in college, meaning it would only be a sheer accident if your assignment worked out to five appropriate paragraphs. Your high school teachers taught you this method to help you see your writing as parts that complete a whole, but this strategy does not work with longer pieces of writing, writing that includes dialogue, writing that explains any process in more than five steps, and so forth. Imagine, if your history professor assigns you a 10-page paper—and he or she will at some point—how many pages your paragraphs would have to be to apply to this rule!

- **How long should my paragraphs be?**

Though there are no rules about paragraph length, the rule that only one idea can appear in a paragraph typically keeps our paragraphs in check so they are neither too short nor do they ramble. Basically, a short paragraph should not be less than 50 words, and a long paragraph should not be more than 250 words or half of a typed page.

- **When do I end one paragraph and begin another?**

After you have explained all the information relating to the topic sentence and provided a conclusion to the material, you should exit and begin the next idea.

- **Do I have to indent every paragraph?**

Unless you are writing a letter in which everything is left justified and you skip double lines between the single-spaced sentences, all paragraphs must be indented. The easiest way to indent is by using the Tab key on your keyboard.

- **Can I change the order of sentences after I write a paragraph?**

Absolutely! During revision, which we discuss in depth in Chapter 18, you should always consider how sentence order affects your paragraph's meaning. Most writers move sentences around quite liberally until they are satisfied.

Technology Toolbox

Keyboard Composing Advantages

You will save yourself a tremendous amount of time and energy by writing all of your drafts on the computer instead of in longhand to be typed later. This technique, called "keyboard composing," lets you take advantage of your word processor's abilities. For example, when you want to rearrange sentences within a paragraph, you simply drag your mouse over the sentence to highlight it, and, depending on your preferences, either right click to "cut" the sentence or go up to the menu toolbar at the top of the screen under "Edit" to choose "Cut." After you have cut the selected material, simply place your curser to the new location and either right click or go to "Edit" and "paste" the sentence.

Remember to save each of your drafts as a separate file to help you keep account of your changes and to submit to your professors when required. For a single paper you might have First Draft.doc, Second Draft.doc, Final Draft.doc

Topic Sentences

A topic sentence is a complete sentence that discusses in detail the issues covered in the paragraph.

Think of the topic sentence as the map that guides your readers through your paragraph. Without the map or plan, your audience must work extra hard to comprehend your work. With the map they can concentrate on your meaning without constantly reassessing the structure and style.

Authors might omit topic sentences because they forget the needs of the intended audience and neglect to share the information. In other words, writing is such a cerebral activity that authors often fail to remember that their audiences are not as familiar with the work, have not conducted the same research, and are not as fluent in the subject matter.

An easy way to write a topic sentence or a thesis statement (see Chapter 15) in your rough draft is to use this beginning: "In this paragraph I will discuss. . ." *Before you submit your draft to your professor or to your peers for review, go back and edit out this helper introduction.*

Creating a Topic Sentence

As you will see in Exercise 13.1 at the end of this chapter, one topic sentence reads: "Though it has been an ongoing problem for centuries, domestic violence is still not discussed often in literature."

In an earlier draft, the author knew she wanted to express her opinion that most literary authors avoid the topic of domestic violence before she used Zora Neale Hurston's short story, "Sweat" to support her thesis, but she went through a few tries before arriving at the final topic sentence.

First, she found her topic: Domestic violence in Hurston's "Sweat."

Then she drafted a few topic sentences for her first paragraph:

Too general:	Domestic violence does not exist in today's literature.
Too specific:	Zora Neale Hurston is one of the only authors willing to discuss domestic violence in literature.
Appropriate:	Though it has been an ongoing problem for centuries, domestic violence is still not discussed often in literature.

Making Appropriate Topic Sentences

Issue/Topic	Topic Sentence
Online gaming	People should blame the individuals and not the games for the negative effects of the habit.
Global warming	The ice floes in Antarctica are melting more rapidly than scientists previously thought.
Gas prices	Gas prices will never dip below $2 a gallon again.

Transitions: Create Paragraphs Using Time, Spatial, or Logical Order

Transitions are words or phrases that establish relationships between sentences and paragraphs by linking; connecting; signaling a change of direction or other movement; and creating an order by time, space, or logic.

To help you understand the importance of transitions, think about when you take a friend to a new place, like another friend's house for a party, you are the transition for your friend. You introduce her to people, maybe give her a tour of the house, and generally make sure she does not get lost in unfamiliar surroundings. In your writing, transitions offer the same services to your readers who are unfamiliar with your paragraphs.

Provide a concession:
Admittedly, the prosecution would feel more comfortable with witnesses.

Indicate causes or effects:
Since no one has come forward as an eyewitness, consequently, the prosecution must work with what it has at this point.

Use these and any of the transitions listed in the table between paragraphs, too.

Level 1

Name _____ **Date** _____

DIRECTIONS The following sentences make a rough draft of a paragraph, but the sentences are out of order. In the blank to the right, identify each sentence as a topic, support, or concluding sentence. Then rewrite the sentences in the space below as a paragraph with the topic sentence at the beginning, followed by support, and then the conclusion.

1. Writers avoid the topic because it is taboo to some extent and it raises some uncomfortable issues. _____

   _____

2. Sykes and Delia Jones are in a miserable union in which Sykes makes it a daily habit to abuse his wife both physically and mentally. _____

   _____

3. Though it has been an ongoing problem for centuries, domestic violence is still not discussed often in literature. _____

   _____

4. So why does Sykes beat Delia, and more importantly, why does Delia stay with her abusive husband? _____

   _____

5. Zora Neale Hurston moves into this habitually avoided territory with her short story entitled "Sweat." _____

   _____

6. Furthermore, is Delia's inaction to save her husband at the end of the story morally reprehensible? _____

   _____

Level 1

Name_____ **Date**_____

DIRECTIONS Following are several concept clusters that will eventually function as paragraphs about the importance of bee hives. Read through the information and in the blank below each one, write an appropriate topic sentence that would sustain a well-formed paragraph.

1. Bees make honey and store it in wax catacombs in the hive.

   The bees use the honey as a food source during the winter when flowers do not bloom.

   European honey bees make more honey than the bees in the hive need.

   Most hives around the world have European honey bees.

   _____

2. The queen is the leader of the bee hive and its largest member.

   Drones are the next largest members of the hive.

   Worker bees are the smallest members of the hive.

   _____

3. The queen is selected by drones at birth.

   She kills competing females.

   She mates with drones to keep the hive healthy.

   Queen bees can lay up to 1500 eggs per day.

   _____

4. Worker bees make the honeycomb where the honey is stored.

   They gather pollen from plants and flowers.

   They defend the hive from outside invasion.

   Then clean the hive and tend to the queen.

   _____

Level 1

Name _____ **Date**_____

DIRECTIONS Read the following clusters and determine in the blank provided the correct transitional method (chronological, spatial, or logical). Underline all the order words or phrases that you identify in the sentences.

SAMPLE

There are <u>several reasons</u> why Janet likes reality TV shows like *Survivor*. <u>First,</u> she loves the physical challenges. <u>Then</u> there are the mental games people play with each other. <u>On a par with that</u> are the exotic locations. *Chronological* _____

1. Mary loves shows about animals, particularly ones where a camera takes the audience into a nest or up a tree. Recently, scientists attached a camera to a large spider. Spidercam's images showed a narrow tunnel that became smaller toward the end. At the end was a large mud room about 2 feet tall and equally wide. On the left side of the space two other spiders cowered against the wall at the intruder who kept the tunnel immediately behind him for a fast getaway. _____

2. One of the first reality shows ever was MTV's *Real World*. Contestants auditioned for the opportunity to live with strangers in a house outfitted with cameras. The concept however caught on with American watchers because *Real World* has been on the air for 21 years. Subsequently, many other reality shows have attempted to cash in on *Real World's* popularity. *Survivor*, for instance, is a successful example of the phenomenon. Not all reality shows make the grade although. *Playing it Straight* and *My Big, Fat Obnoxious Boss* could not catch popular ratings. Consequently, television producers are watchful about which shows they decide to run. _____

3. In 1990 *Northern Exposure* introduced viewers to a quirky bunch of transplants and local Native Americans living in Cicely, Alaska. It was an instant success because at that time no show came close to the sharp dialogue, interesting plots, and colorful characters. The show's main character, Dr. Joel Fleischman, is a New Yorker who finds himself paying off student loans by working in Alaska. At first Fleischman is resistant to the townspeople's charms, but eventually he warms to them. Until he does, he is constantly at odds with the lead female character, Maggie O'Connell, which perpetuates their tension. Meanwhile, Chris Stevens, the local DJ, reads poetry and existential literature on air, Holling Vincour and Shelley Tambo run the town's pub, and Ed Chigliak is a 21-year old local who personally knows film great Martin Scorsese. Until its demise in 1995, *Northern Exposure* represented some of the best television. _____

4. My favorite television night is Wednesday because *Lost* is followed by *CSI Las Vegas*. That provides viewers with back to back excitement but on different levels. On *Lost* the characters constantly battle "The Others" who are nearby, but far enough away to keep our heroes guessing. Last season they found the hatch, an underground building that not

only answered questions about the island but created more. Next to *Lost, CSI* offers suspense on a different level. The investigators must cover a crime scene so thoroughly that they become a part of it by crawling under cars, collecting evidence in between a victim's fingernails, and other meticulous circumstances. Sometimes the investigators themselves are victims, such as the season finale when Nick Stokes was kidnapped and put in an underground coffin. _____

Level 1

Name _____ **Date**_____

DIRECTIONS The following paragraph contains no transitions. Using your two transition charts found in this workbook and *The Thomson Handbook,* provide transitions to narrow the focus, introduce conclusions or summaries, signal concession, or provide cause and effect. Rearrange the wording and the sentences to suit your revision.

    Most people harbor dreams of becoming musical stars. It may begin in our bedrooms while we sing along to the radio and play air instruments. Some study a musical instrument and start their own bands. Garage bands are pretty common and at least one person probably knows two or three people in these start-up groups. They might be rock, alternative, hip hop, country, or other styles. Some bands are lucky enough to make the transition from the garage to the club scene. If they do well in local clubs, meaning establish themselves with their fans, they may succeed in touring in limited areas. The small bands who make it to the next level usually have a solid fan base of people willing to travel within a small radius to hear them play. To succeed in general playing live is not enough. Bands serious about moving up need CDs to promote themselves with their fans, get airplay on the radio, and get a manager or public relations expert. A few find themselves moving to big cities known for music such as New York, Nashville, Chicago, and Los Angeles. The national music industry is the hardest level to break into and takes the most effort and money.

_____

_____

_____

_____

_____

_____

_____

_____

_____

_____

_____

Level 2

Name _____ **Date** _____

DIRECTIONS Following are ideas for a paper. Using your two transition charts and the information you've read in this workbook and *The Thomson Handbook,* revise the ideas into topic sentences and then write the paragraphs.

Topic: fruit trees on campus

Audience: campus administration

Purpose: to convince the audience to plant apple, pear, and peach trees instead of ornamental flowering trees.

Paragraph One: explain how students could eat healthy and cheaply from fruit trees.

Paragraph Two: discuss how fruit trees are no more expensive than ornamentals currently on campus.

Paragraph Three: describe how students and faculty would benefit and the university would be in the forefront of new ideas in the nation.

Writing within Established Contexts

The Thomson Handbook, **Chapters 1, 7, 9–13**

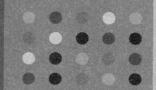

Defined Purposes and Specified Audiences

Purpose

Most critics believe the difference between a successful and an unsuccessful ad campaign, letter to the editor, memo to the executive committee, paper for English composition, online posting forum, and other forms of written communication boils down to the author's ability to tailor the message to a specific **audience** (instead of a general one or the person who assigned the piece) and express a crisply defined **purpose.**

Mapping out a **purpose,** your reason for writing or what you want to accomplish with your writing, should not be unduly foreign to you because you also express your purpose in your **thesis statement** or any **claims** you make. Early in your writing experience your teacher may have assisted you in identifying your purpose with the helping phrase:

In this paper I will prove . . . in which you define what you will prove.

In this paper I will prove that long distance relationships can work under certain conditions.

As a college-level writer, you no longer need that helping phrase:

Long distant relationships can work under certain circumstances.

As you will see below, your **purpose** is dependent upon the **genre** and the **audience.** **Purpose** has been classified into four categories:

- *Reflection or expression:* subjective writing where your purpose may be to share your feelings, thoughts, and ideas through informal genres like memoirs, journal or diary entries, personal correspondence like letter writing, blogging, email, or other online venues like *Facebook, Xanga,* or *MySpace.*

    Perhaps I am just part of the curious minority that refuses to judge a Web site by its home page (could that be the new cliché for the technologically advanced and obsessed twenty-first century?), but if I really care about what a site has to offer me, I am certainly not going to banish it from my bookmarks because the home page does not measure up to my standards, standards that are subjective and therefore can never be completely realized. (Melanie Beahm, Journal homework response)

- *Information:* writing to inform occupies much of our scholarly discourse, and is objective writing whereas reflecting is subjective writing. We read informative writing in textbooks, newspapers, magazines, journals, Web sites, and so forth. Informative writing defines and explains to clarify concepts and ideas for readers. Anything from a recipe for New Orleans style gumbo to an article about space exploration in Saturn's rings is considered informative writing.

College students from Morocco and Algeria are learning about American culture by spending the month of July at Christopher Newport University. In addition to classroom learning, the 20 North African students at CNU will learn about American history and government, American culture and Virginia's ecology through excursions and site visits. They also will learn about leadership and volunteerism and have opportunities to strengthen their English-language speaking and writing skills. Twenty CNU students will live and study with the North African students, who will be on the CNU campus from July 2 to July 30. (News Release, June 29, 2006)

- *Persuasion:* whereas reflection is subjective and information is objective, persuasion is a combination of the two styles that is used to impress and convince readers to adopt a new position or change a current opinion. In traditional persuasive or argumentative writing, authors present two opposing sides while giving greater weight to their preferred views. Persuasive writing appears in newspaper editorials, opinion pieces found in print and online, scholarly journals in which the author attempts to convince readers to see evidence as compelling in one way, a blog in which the author rants against an issue, an email where the writer asks for an extension on a paper, and so forth. Because persuasive discourse can be reflective or informative, it is one of the most pervasive and popular writing styles.

People all over the world tend to think the conflict in Iraq is hopeless and will end in a bitter civil war, destroying the country and the people that occupy it. Iraq is not hopeless though, it is merely frustrated. Iraq will find the peace and freedom that it has dreamed of for so long, primarily because of the hope that is left in the youth, culture, and countries like America that are helping fight for it. (Boone Brosseseau, "Iraq: Frustrated But Not Hopeless," March 28, 2006).

- *Evaluation:* like persuasion, evaluation can be a combination of reflection and information in which the author reviews, evaluates, reports, or critiques an event, book, film, concert, reading, play, speech, rally, or other event or product. The author must use a set of criteria that measures merits, abilities, techniques, services, and so forth. We see evaluation typically in arts and entertainment reviews, and your professors may ask you to attend or watch an event and submit your own evaluation.

The existence of racial hate crimes is not exposed in every culture, although it does secretly thrive in them all. *American History X* was produced in 1998 with the intentions of making a lasting impression on the general public about the significance of racial hatred and inequality in America. The film provides an opportunity for cultures to observe severe racial issues without having to experience the troubling ethos firsthand. *American History X* is a life changing motion picture because it ruthlessly exposes the viewer to the disturbing violent acts among races, it illustrates how Derek's mistakes ruin the rest of the family's lifestyle, and shows that the humanity of former rivals emits hope for altering Derek—and ultimately Danny's—racial outlook. (Julie Johnson, "Graced with a Second Chance," October 15, 2004)

Audience and Tone

Any time you write something to submit or be read by others, you create public discourse (Chapter 12), and you must write deliberately to an **audience** using the most appropriate **tone** for the **purpose.**

How many times have you read a Web site or a print article and wondered, "What the heck was that about?" You may have blamed the author for using terms and a tone that were too technical or advanced or chided yourself for not being sophisticated enough for the material. However, the miscommunication probably occurred because you were simply not the intended audience.

Likewise, how often when writing email do you use emoticons, those happy faces, or find yourself writing parenthetical statements like (just kidding) or (seriously)? Email is one of the few forums where **tone,** the attitude and mood you apply to your writing, gets murky or misunderstood.

During your college career your professors will require you to select an intended audience and to write specifically to that individual or group. Here are a few examples:

- *Yourself.* When you write a homework response or journal entry, your instructors expect you to write informally, use first person, and be honest. In the example above about a reflective piece, student Melanie Beahm begins her response by identifying herself within a group whose ideals she shares, which is helpful for her audience—herself—to then rationalize about her beliefs, and her professor to put into context Melanie's observations. Her tone is honest, frank, and a little argumentative to indicate she disagrees with material in the homework assignment.

- *Your peers.* Many times you will be asked to read and respond to a classmate's writing, as well as submit your work to the same process. The most effective peer responses combine honest observations in a friendly and informal, but serious tone. If you know the person well or are worried you may hurt some feelings, you may end your evaluation with a friendly note like, "I know these comments are causing you a lot of work, and if you want me to read your revisions, let me know." That way you insure your comments are not misconstrued as mean-spirited. Empty superlatives like "Great job!" ring hollow and are ineffective. Also, since you know your work will be received by an audience larger than just your professor, you should consider whether the material is offensive or too controversial for a group.

If you write a letter to the school newspaper, your audience is essentially all students. In this context, your tone should be knowledgeable and demonstrate your passion and commitment to the issue.

- *Your professors.* Many times your professors do not assign audiences, so you know they are your intended readers. In these cases, your job is to demonstrate you understand the material and can engage the concepts with your own writing. In doing so, they evaluate you on your critical reading skills, ability to analyze and repackage new concepts in your own words, write within the standards of formal writing such as correct usage and grammar, effectively document ideas and sources other than your own by using proper procedures, and situate your work within a specific academic discourse community.

Create Tone to Match Your Audience and Purpose

We use attitude, mood, and language to establish **tone** with our readers. In some cases our choices say, "Don't mess with me today!" while other times we evoke an "I am an authority on this issue," with language and attitude.

Some Attitudes, Moods, and Emotions in Academic Writing

awed	exuberant	interested	satirical
curious	friendly	ironic	serious
dismissive	hesitant	knowledgeable	skeptical
doubtful	indifferent	playful	submissive
entertaining	instructional	reflective	sympathetic

Consider these two emails:

Hey Dr. Wright,

Yo, whatup? I came by your office earlier but you must have been out playing or drinking coffee or something, ha ha! Anyway, I was wondering if you would be willing to write a letter of recommendation for me for graduate school. I know you will write fabulous things about me and tell them they better take me, right?

Your favorite student ever,

Joey Cole

Dear Dr. Wright,

I came by your office today to check on office hours, and to find the best time to see you. I would like to make an appointment for next Tuesday, March 5, at 1:00. As we discussed in our last meeting, I am interested in applying for graduate school and would be honored if you would write me a letter of recommendation.

Since I have taken two classes with you and enjoyed many discussions after class regarding my plans, I look forward to planning this important phase of my career with you.

Best,

Joey Cole

The differences between the first and second emails are found in attitude, tone, and language use. In the first, the student takes too many liberties with his professor, no matter how well the two know each other. Though email is less formal than other forms of writing, Joey's slang and the way he assumes Dr. Wright will gladly write him a letter are too forward. In the second email, Joey is respectful, considerate of his professor's schedule and time, and reminds her that his graduate school plans are something in which they have a shared interest.

Using Evidence to Support Your Claims

Most of the formal writing you will do in college requires you to **support** or prove your **claims** or assertions. Even when you write a homework response to an outside reading in which you state your opinion, your professors will want you to back up that observation with evidence from the text.

Technology Toolbox

Keeping Track of Online Research URLs

When conducting research online, always copy the url (uniform resource locator) address because you will need the information for in-text citations and Works Cited or Bibliography pages.

Before you begin searching online, make a new document called *Sources* to collect all the urls. Keep that document open during your online searches so you can copy and paste between the Web page you are on and your source page easily. To copy the url, put your mouse in the address block and click once to highlight the address. Then on your keyboard choose Ctrl + C, which is the copy command.

At the bottom of the screen you should see your sources page. Click on that to bring up the page, find the appropriate spot, and Ctrl + V pastes the url. After you hit Enter, the url turns blue, which means the word processing program has made it a link.

Once you have finished your exploratory research, use the source page to return to the pages.

Whether you are responding to a homework assignment or writing a formal research paper, you must supply **evidence** from outside sources to **support your claims,** beliefs, observations, or assertions. Without outside sources, your work lacks credibility because every observation can be nothing more than an opinion. Consider how suspicious the following claims are without evidence:

- Global warming poses an immense threat to all life on Earth. *(Really? Says who?)*
- People who do not vote should not voice their opinions about our elected leaders. *(Who are you to tell everyone else what to do?)*
- Convicted rapists should be castrated. *(On what grounds do you make that assertion?)*

One of the biggest problems college students face is when to document their sources. Basically, the best rule of thumb is to **document** anything you did not already know before the writing assignment.

Incorrect:

The Godfather is filled with lessons for life. *(This is an idea found in Sarah Vowell's Take the Cannoli on page 59)*

Correct:

According to author Sarah Vowell, *The Godfather* is filled with lessons for life (59).

Incorrect:

What is interesting about writers and their readers is the margin of overlap we have, meaning those shared experiences, knowledge, beliefs, terminologies, desires, and physical needs. *(plagiarized almost word for word from p. 192 in* The Thomson Handbook)

Correct:

One of the most interesting things I found from last night's reading was how writers and readers share a "margin of overlap," meaning we "share shared experiences, knowledge, beliefs, terminologies, desires, and physical needs" (Blakesley 192).

For more information about proper source citation go to Chapter 17 in *The Thomson Handbook Workbook* and Part Four in *The Thomson Handbook.*

The Academic Genres

In addition to selecting a **purpose** and an **audience,** the final aspect in writing a paper is choosing the appropriate **academic genre,** which governs the type or style of writing. For a complete list of genres and their purposes, see Chapter 7 in *The Thomson Handbook.*

On many occasions your professors or superiors may choose the genre for you, but often you make that choice for yourself. For instance, when your history professor assigns you a midterm paper in which you must cover the impact of one particular battle in the Vietnam War, you have multiple possibilities:

Genre	Audience	Purpose	Style
Argument	anti-war protestors	show how protesting hurt American soldiers who had no choice	sympathetic/ authoritative
Interview/ Narrative	students in class	persuade students to support Vietnam Vet Organization	instructional

Genre	Audience	Purpose	Style
Analytical essay	state senators/congress	demonstrate need for Government funds for VA hospitals	informative

If given the opportunity to pick your audience, purpose, and style as well as your genre, in your prewriting stage make a chart like the one above and work on several completely different combinations before settling on the one you feel best suits the assignment. If you have any doubts, consult your professor with the chart for another opinion.

Level 1

Name_____ **Date**_____

DIRECTIONS Read each of the following examples, and identify in the space beneath the audience, purpose, and tone. Then rewrite for an entirely different audience using a different tone (choose from the list in Chapter 14 or create one of your own).

SAMPLE

First you dip your knife in the peanut butter jar. Then you slather a big slab of the delicious stuff on a slice of bread. Wipe the knife clean by using the bread or your tongue (but don't tell mom). Then dip the knife in the jam jar, preferably grape or strawberry. Slather the gob on the other piece of bread. Smash them together and take a big bite!

Audience: younger sibling because language is playful. Purpose: instruct how to make a p.b.j. Tone is humorous.

Assemble jars of peanut butter and jam, a loaf of bread, a knife, a plate, and a napkin. Open both jars. Open bread container and lay 2 slices side by side. Insert the knife into the peanut butter and scoop a serving size of about 2 tablespoons. Spread evenly on bread. Clean knife of peanut butter residue by raking on jar lip and using napkin to catch remaining spread, and insert into jam jar to scoop 2 tablespoons. Spread evenly on bread. Place slices together and use knife to cut sandwich in half.

Audience: intelligent adult because language is sophisticated. Purpose: how to make a p.b.j. Tone: instructional.

1. Hey Professor Soud, this is your favorite student of all times, ha ha. I am emailing you because I did not turn in my paper when I was supposed to, my bad! The reason is because my roommate sprained her ankle and I drove her to the e.r. where we stayed for like 5 hours. When I finally got back to my room I was so tired so I went to bed and then slept through class. So, what should I do?

_____

_____

_____

_____

2. The homework assignment was very difficult and I found myself reading the same sentences over and over trying to figure out what the author meant. It seems as though he is saying that the environment is in bad trouble and that we are all responsible for fixing the problem, but I could be way off. One thing I liked a lot was his examples, like how

the Chesapeake Bay is literally dead in some places. How can a bay be dead in spots? That is crazy, but that fact really stuck out for me and convinced me there is a big problem we need to solve, and that is how to save Mother Earth.

_____

_____

_____

_____

3. As I began to ask them questions about their work lives, it occurred to me how interesting it is to explore a phenomenon that happens in so many households: one spouse works outside of the home, while the other works inside the home, raising a family and maintaining a home. Unfortunately, many do not give homemaking the recognition it deserves as a profession. It is absolutely a profession. Those who stay at home to raise a family put in an equal, if not larger share of time than their spouse.

_____

_____

_____

_____

4. The *argiope aurantia*, otherwise known as the "writing spider," is a common spider found from Canada through the contiguous 48 states and down as far as Costa Rica. This particular species' common name comes from the zig-zag impression the animal creates at the center of its web. Like most spiders, the female is considerably larger than the male. These spiders are carnivorous and catch their prey in webs that can span as much as 24 inches. *Argiope aurantia* dies at the first hard frost, but leaves at least one brown papery egg sack to winter over. This spider is essential to the environment because it helps keep the insect population in check.

_____

_____

_____

_____

Level 1

Name_____ **Date**_____

DIRECTIONS Revise the following sources of evidence by blending with your wording to make complete sentences.

SAMPLE

Professor Thomas Doubtworthy believes Christopher Marlowe wrote some plays credited to William Shakespeare.

Some scholars like Professor Thomas Doubtworthy believe that William Shakespeare did not write all the plays he has been credited with, and Christopher Marlowe may have written some.

1. The Secret Society for the Santa Anna Winds maintains the winds are responsible for global warming.

   _____

   _____

2. Boston Baked Beans candy is not a bean nor are they baked in Boston, according to Madge Farnsworthy.

   _____

   _____

3. In 2006 Adeline became the first German Shepherd to swim the Potomac River, according to eyewitnesses.

   _____

   _____

4. Gail Rigney's recent book on childcare revolutionized babysitting in America.

   _____

   _____

5. Lorraine Hall's work on the Myers Briggs test shows how personality traits dramatically affect student success.

_____

_____

Level 1

Name_____ **Date**_____

DIRECTIONS In each of the following scenarios the genre and assignment have been provided. Choose the best audience, purpose, and tone, and write a sentence to explain your choice and to demonstrate that you understand the genre. Be creative.

SAMPLE

Write a reflective journal response about the Wounded Knee Massacre of 1890.

My audience will be my classmates, my purpose will be to explain how my appreciation for the American Indian has increased since reading about Wounded Knee, and my tone will be reverent and honorable.

1. Write a case study about bipolar disorder.

   _____

   _____

2. Write a personal essay about a local no-kill animal shelter.

   _____

   _____

3. Write an interview about a family member's greatest accomplishment.

   _____

   _____

4. Write a business letter to apply for a job.

   _____

   _____

5. Write a multimedia presentation about the sunflower.

   _____

   _____

6. Write an oral presentation about the Hope Diamond.

   _____

   _____

7. Write a proposal about banning cell phones on airplanes.

   _____

   _____

Level 2

Name_____ **Date**_____

DIRECTIONS Using the list on p. 125 in *The Thomson Handbook,* choose the best genre, and list audience, purpose, and tone for each of the following writing assignments; then write a sentence to explain your choice. You will have to conduct Internet research on many of these topics, so include the url with your answers.

SAMPLE

Assignment: write about one element about the assassination of President John F. Kennedy.

Genre: argument, audience: Warren Commission, purpose: persuade the commission to reopen the investigation, tone: firm and instructive.

The audience must be someone who has the power to actually do something other than agree with me, and I want to argue that the commission's findings differ greatly from other historical findings.

1. Write about a professor in your university.

   _____

   _____

2. Explore the origins of soil.

   _____

   _____

3. Discuss the importance of common table salt.

   _____

   _____

4. Write about the Lakota Indian histories called "Winter Counts."

   _____

   _____

5. Explore one species found on the Galapagos Islands.

   _____

   _____

6. Explain the work of Eadweard Muybridge.

   _____

   _____

7. Discuss your favorite pizza toppings and restaurant.

   _____

   _____

8. Investigate the lighthouses located in the Great Lakes.

   _____

   _____

9. Write a report on Ralph Ellison.

   _____

   _____

10. Explain the significance of the San Andreas Fault line.

    _____

    _____

11. Write about chewing gum.

    _____

    _____

12. Explain how ultrasound works.

    _____

    _____

Writing Thesis Statements

The Thomson Handbook, Chapters 4, 14

A **thesis statement** is one or sometimes two sentences that clearly identify the main points of your project.

Perhaps no other element in your paper is more important than your **thesis** because it guides your readers by giving them a map showing what they can expect in your paper. Therefore, the rule of thumb about a thesis statement is if you do not list the issue in your thesis, it should not appear in your paper.

Think of your thesis as the rest of this sentence:

(In this paper I will specifically discuss) _____

For example:

> Calexico State needs a marching band to provide music during sporting events, give greater opportunities to music students, and bring prominence to the university.

Simply by reading this thesis statement we know exactly what the author plans to discuss and what will not be part of the paper. Therefore, if we read later in the paper that a drawback to the marching band is the expense for uniforms and instruments, we will instantly know the author has strayed from the thesis. If the paper is still in a rough draft form, we can suggest that the author revise the thesis to include opposition:

> Calexico State needs a marching band to provide music during sporting events, give greater opportunities to music students, and bring prominence to the university; however, such a program will be very expensive to fund and maintain, due to uniform and musical instrument cost and upkeep.

Well before you articulate a thesis statement, you will have conducted much of the research and preparation explained in Chapter 14 of *The Thomson Handbook*.

- *Think ahead.* Plan your time well and establish a realistic timeline in your day planner. At this point you should have your assignment.

- *Explore the subject matter.* Talk to friends and your professors, conduct a few tentative searches for sources, and explore your interests in brainstorming activities.

- *Focus on the subject.* Ask your reference librarian to help you narrow the field, and have fun simply exploring your subject before you begin to see how you can offer insights into what you selected.

- *Develop a hypothesis,* which may or may not resemble your thesis later. Write out a tentative plan for how you will personally impact the subject matter.

- *Plan your research.* Armed with the hypothesis, begin narrowing the focus from the very broad topic to a specific issue. At this point some of the issues you plan to discuss in your thesis and paper should be emerging from the material.

- *Find background information.* Like a good detective, find what you can about your topic from sources you have not consulted. What big names in the field are talking about your research, and in what sources?

- *Keep a research journal.* Personalize the journal to best suit your work style, but make sure you record your movements, where you have been, what you have read.

- *Record bibliographic information.* Whether in note cards or in a separate word processing document, record all sources you have read or plan to read. This can be as easy as pasting Web addresses in a file and labeling it "Paper Sources."

- *Create a working annotated bibliography.* This tool will help you when you begin writing because at a glance you can see how to organize your paper based upon your findings.

- *Establish your authority.* No matter how interesting or important the research you gather, make sure your voice dominates over the cluttered conversation in your paper. Your readers are interested in what **you** have to say, how **you** view the subject matter, and **your** addition to the scholarly conversation.

By completing these important steps you should be able to move easily from the **assignment** to the **topic** to the **thesis statement.**

Assignment	Topic	Thesis Statement
Write an argument about a campus issue.	campus recycling	The administration should hire a recycling service because paper from departments, plastics from the dining hall, and cans and bottles from the dorms are going in the landfills instead of being recycled.
Write a research paper about a spider we studied in this earth science unit.	writing spider	The writing spider is a beneficial member of any garden because it catches flies and other pests, is not poisonous, and makes its home in plants to avoid human contact.

From Statement to Thesis Statement

Most authors go through the various writing stages suggested in Chapter 14 of *The Thomson Handbook* and still fall just short of the thesis statement because they make an **observation** or **factual statement** but not a **thesis** based on ideas they have formed through research.

Observations are good beginnings. However, notice in the following examples how the observation is sound but does not provide enough information; this causes your readers to work or struggle to understand your meaning:

Something needs to be done about waste on our campus. *(What needs to be done and for what reasons? What kind of waste?)*

Spiders are *good for the environment. (Probably so, but why? Are some better for the environment than others?)*

It is important to *travel. (Who should travel and why is it important?)*

August Wilson is a brilliant playwright. *(Certainly so, but on which grounds do you base this judgment?)*

If the issue is important enough to appear in the most important sentence of your paper, it warrants enough attention to be explicitly stated.

Avoid generalities and unclear statements because they do not express the reasons why you proposed your thesis—which will surely make up the bulk of your paper. Ask yourself why the statement is important and chances are you will see you left out some of the details.

Let the Thesis Create a Map of Your Paper

If written well, your thesis will help you outline the contents of each paragraph of your paper:

Thesis:
Potential recruits must understand how their decision to join the military affects not only their lives, but also those of their family, friends, and loved ones, so the choice should be made only after much discussion.

Outline:
  I. Introduction: Many people who want to enlist in the military make the decision quickly and before talking with their families.
  II. Consider about how your life will change.
  III. Understand how the choice will affect parents, spouses, children.
  IV. The choice will impact friends.
  V. Conclusion/Resolution: before enlisting, have many discussions with all important people in your life.

Your thesis also will keep you on target and prevent you from straying off topic:

Thesis:
Potential recruits must understand how their decision to join the military affects not only their lives, but also those of their family, friends, and loved ones, so the choice should be made only after much discussion.

Outline:
  I. Introduction: Many people who want to enlist in the military make the decision quickly and before talking with their families.
  II. Consider about how your life will change.
  III. *Jobs and college opportunities will have to wait.*
  IV. Understand how the choice will affect parents, spouses, children.
  V. The choice will impact friends.
  VI. Conclusion/Resolution: before enlisting, have many discussions with all important people in your life.

Notice that III discusses an issue off the topic, demonstrating how the thesis and the outline can work together. If you find yourself adding information to your outline that does not exist in the thesis, simply revise the thesis to reflect the new material:

Potential recruits must understand how their decision to join the military affects not only their lives, *such as employment and educational opportunities that will be put on hold*, but also those of their family, friends, and loved ones, so the choice should be made only after much discussion.

Let Your Outline Guide Your Thesis

Many professors require students to write an outline or a list of concepts that will be covered in the paper before creating the thesis or beginning the paper. This technique helps prevent students from writing about ideas that stray from a solid, well-thought-out plan.

Outline for Argument Rough Draft

Subject: Professional Athletes in Olympic Games

Audience: International Olympic Committee (IOC)

Purpose: Persuade the committee to ban professional athletes from competing in the games.

I. Introduction: where and when first games began, who competed, for what purpose
II. Athletes were "gentlemen" and their sports considered noble
III. History should prevail as games were amateur until 1970s
IV. Amateur athletes keep politics out of the games
V. Amateur athletes keep greed out of the games
VI. Opposition: amateur rules are unfair and limiting. Times have changed.
VII. Rebuttal: professional athletes are unfair and limiting. What does time have to do with the argument?
VIII. Conclusion: restore amateur-only requirements to return Olympics to a focus on human endurance and athleticism, not corporate greed and national boasting.

Though probably too elaborate for an argument paper that is 4–5 pages, a preliminary thesis statement might look like this:

The International Olympic Committee should reinstate amateur-only rules to restore the focus to human endurance and athleticism because currently the games are weakened by politics and greed.

Thesis Sentence Style Options

Like any sentence you write, the thesis must follow typical grammatical conventions, but there are no hard rules about style and sentence construction. However, most thesis sentences are **complex,** contain **subordinate phrases,** and are very **specific.**

As we covered in Chapter 9, the **complex thesis statement** incorporates independent and dependent clauses to **coordinate** and **subordinate** ideas expressed in the sentence. Since some parts of your thesis may be more important than other ideas, you may create a statement with a main clause and a subordinate clause:

SUB. CLAUSE   MAIN CLAUSE AND THESIS

Although expensive, pomegranate juice is loaded with the heart-healthy antioxidants, cancer-fighting ingredients, and anti-aging properties.

MAIN CLAUSE AND THESIS

Because pomegranate juice is loaded with the heart-healthy antioxidants, cancer-fighting ingredients, and anti-aging properties, many find the juice worth the extra expense.

SUBORDINATE CLAUSE

If your thesis becomes too awkward as a single sentence, consider two main clauses with a semicolon:

> Pomegranate juice is loaded with the heart-healthy antioxidants, cancer-fighting ingredients, and anti-aging properties; therefore, health-conscious consumers or those with a family history of heart disease and or cancer should consume the juice regularly.

Matching Discipline and Genre to Thesis Statement Styles

Chapter 7 of *The Thomson Handbook* presented the different academic genres you will be learning in your classes. Though thesis statements are basically the same across the disciplines, there are specific requirements to remember.

Discipline	Genre	Thesis Expectations
Government	Review an article	Critically evaluate the article based on personal opinion and evidence in article
Physics	Lab Report	Make a brief statement of main purpose (to observe, conduct experiment, etc.)
Psychology	Comparison Paper of two articles	State the main points and claims of each article
Anthropology	Case Study	Clearly state issues and make recommendations for solution
Computer Science	Argument	State main claim, evidence, opposition
Philosophy	Critique	Critically analyze a single author or piece of writing using evidence from the text for support
English	Compare/Contrast	Critically analyze main points of agreement and disagreement in each text

This chart provides some examples of what you may encounter in your college writing assignments, but most of your professors will give you detailed instructions to follow. When in doubt, double check.

Each discipline requires a fairly distinct style, with exception to the research paper, which stays remarkably similar across the courses. In a research paper, your main job is to identify a concept within a topic and provide extenuating research to support your own claim (see Chapter 17 in *The Thomson Handbook Workbook*).

Thesis Checklist

Whether you create an outline first and a thesis second, or thesis first and an outline second, there are certain elements that simply do not belong in this mighty sentence or two.

A good thesis contains:

- A clear description of the main idea or the central issue
- Your purpose, whether you are defending, arguing, presenting, or observing
- A very brief description of the supporting material used to define the central issue
- Any opposition to the central idea
- Language and style appropriate to the discipline

Technology Toolbox

Tracking Your Revisions

Because you may adjust your thesis statement and outline from time to time until they fit your purpose, audience, and needs, you should keep track of the changes using your word processor's "Track Changes" function. You can easily see your changes since they will appear in color. You can assign a different color for each draft's revisions to keep a record of every revision you make. For example, as you revise from Draft One to Draft Two, your edits can be red. From Draft Two to Draft Three, you can revise in blue.

Your professors see writing as a process, which means you will submit drafts of your papers to either your professor or classmates for review before the final paper is due. The "Track Changes" option permits you to see any revisions they suggest, and your professors can easily identify the depth of your revisions

Level 1

Name_____ Date_____

DIRECTIONS Read each of the following examples, and identify whether the statement is an observation (O) or a thesis statement (TS). If the statement is an observation, explain why in the space provided.

SAMPLE

The Golden Gate Bridge opened for business on May 28, 1937. *(O)*

This is a fact that shows no relevance other than when the bridge opened. A paper could not exist on the date the bridge opened.

1. The weather conditions and technology at the time made constructing the bridge dangerous.

_____

_____

2. Eleven workers died because of safety malfunctions during the bridge's construction.

_____

_____

3. The Golden Gate Bridge is not painted gold.

_____

_____

4. There are several reasons why the bridge was painted "orange vermillion."

_____

_____

5. Bridge maintenance is ongoing because workers must battle weather and wear and tear to maintain safety.

_____

_____

6. The Golden Gate Bridge appears in many popular movies because of its symbolism.

_____

_____

7. The bridge permits carpooling, pedestrian traffic, and bike traffic as options for area commuters.

_____

_____

8. In this paper I will discuss why the Golden Gate Bridge is interesting.

_____

_____

9. The Golden Gate Bridge is a tourist attraction in addition to the city of San Francisco.

_____

_____

Level 1

Name_____ Date_____

DIRECTIONS Each of the following sentences is an opinion or a statement. In the space provided, revise to create an effective thesis statement.

SAMPLE

A little known fact about the country of Greece is that it has lots of lakes, forests, and other lush vegetation.

Though many think of Greece as arid and dry, tourists can also enjoy exploring the island's many lakes and forests.

1. The Acropolis in Athens is the most sacred spot in the country to many Greeks.

   _____

   _____

2. One of the most important structures in Greece, the Parthenon was built on the Acropolis to honor Parthenos, Athens's patron saint.

   _____

   _____

3. The Temple of Zeus was built around 470 B.C. and is located in Olympus, home of the first Olympic Games.

   _____

   _____

4. Tourists and locals enjoy Greece's 405 beaches and pristine blue waters.

   _____

   _____

5. Though travel in general is expensive, students can travel cheaply in Greece.

   _____

   _____

6. In the summer there are many outdoor activities to enjoy.

_____

_____

7. Traveling within the country has gotten easier in the last decade.

_____

_____

8. The Greek cuisine is much more expansive than what most tourists think.

_____

_____

Level 1

Name_____ **Date**_____

DIRECTIONS Revise the following observations into thesis statements that reflect your opinion.

SAMPLE

People who talk on cell phones in restaurants are rude.

Taking a phone call in a restaurant is inconsiderate to the people you are dining with because you ignore them, you disturb the people around you, and you are not giving the person calling your full attention.

1. AIDS affects everyone.

   _____

   _____

2. Tooth whitening is a safe process.

   _____

   _____

3. Exercise your constitutional right to vote in the next election.

   _____

   _____

4. Spring break should be 10 days long.

   _____

   _____

5. The student government should book more on-campus bands.

   _____

   _____

6. Groundhog Day is an important holiday.

_____

_____

7. Colleges should not have a mandatory laptop requirement.

_____

_____

8. Athletic shoes are too expensive.

_____

_____

9. Every student should be required to take a computer science course.

_____

_____

Level 2

Name_____ **Date**_____

DIRECTIONS A thesis statement should not leave the reader wondering how the author will achieve his or her promise or why this issue is important. Revise the following weak thesis statements into strong ones by answering *how* or *why*. Explain your answer in parentheses.

SAMPLE

Over the years farming in America has changed dramatically.

American farms were once family owned and operated, meaning farmers were not part of a corporation, their children and other relatives worked the land, and the family was responsible for selling the produce and livestock. (There are many ways to approach this issue, but I focused on family owned farms which are rare now.)

1. Statistics prove mammals live longer if they live with a companion animal.

   _____

   _____

2. The U.S. government needs to do more to protect its citizens from terror.

   _____

   _____

3. Before traveling abroad, tourists should learn as much of the language and customs as possible.

   _____

   _____

4. Our public school system needs more funding than ever.

   _____

   _____

5. Studies show that people who abuse alcohol are more likely to abuse other drugs.

_____

_____

6. Every year brushfires in the west seem to worsen.

_____

_____

7. The Grand Canyon was created out of the raging waters of the Colorado River.

_____

_____

8. La Jolla Cove in San Diego, CA offers excellent scuba diving conditions.

_____

_____

9. Genealogy is a fascinating way of learning about family members.

_____

_____

10. Adoption records should remain sealed unless the adopted person and birth parents give consent otherwise.

_____

_____

11. Small businesses could improve their income with a simple Web site.

_____

_____

The Parts of the Essay
The Thomson Handbook, Chapters 2, 4

Like much of what we do, writing is an orderly process, and most writers develop routines or habits in their work. From our earliest papers we were taught that most essays or pieces of writing can be categorized in three chunks: **beginning, middle,** and **end.**

As we honed our skills and our writing became more sophisticated, we discovered that most academic papers come in four to five chunks: **preamble, beginning, middle, end,** and **bibliographic information.**

The Preamble

Writers employ a preamble, also known as a *preface*, to set a tone, provide a scenario, or introduce a theme that they want readers to know prior to beginning with an introduction. Some preambles may be chewy quotations designed to spark thought, and these should be right justified.

> I am the Seven Deadly Sins
>
> Now is it bihovely thyng to telle whiche been the sevene deedly synnes, this is to seyn, chiefaynes of synnes
>
> Geoffrey Chaucer, *The Canterbury Tales*

The first of the seven deadly sins I met turned out to be Anger when, as a child, I became enraged with my new baby brother and tried to scratch his eyes. Of course, looking back I see that Envy played a big part in the drama because I was jealous that he was replacing me as the center of attention in our family.

In this example, the author elects to use Chaucer in his original Middle English dialect for two distinct purposes:

"I wanted Chaucer because he provides terrific credibility and he helps trace the timelessness of the Seven Deadly Sins. In this piece, I focus on how humans are doomed to repeat the sins of the past, and I make it clear that the jealousy I felt at my brother's insertion into our home is what children have always thought through the ages. Second, I could have used Chaucer in translation, but the Middle English dialect echoes that eternal feeling I wanted with this essay."

Some like to begin with a vignette, a short piece to set the tone, mood, and stage. Vignettes can be italicized to remain set off from the rest of the piece:

> An Analysis of the Seven Deadly Sins in the American Family
>
> *The first of the seven deadly sins I met turned out to be Anger when, as a child, I became enraged with my new baby brother and tried to scratch his eyes. Of course, looking back I see that Envy played a big part in the drama because I was jealous that he was replacing me as the center of attention in our family.*
>
> Phil Cignorelli

Research shows how the Seven Deadly Sins actually began as customs and evolved into law in cultures that had little governmental or religious control. First known in ancient Greece, the original sins numbered eight but were later dropped to seven.

In this example, the author wants to create a connection to the academic material with his readers to establish ethos or credibility, but he knows a personal story is not appropriate in a scholarly paper, so he employs the preamble to disseminate his vignette without violating the integrity of the paper.

In academic writing the **preamble** should be used sparingly, and should never be part of the page or word count for an assignment because it exists purely outside of the paper. If you are unsure about this writing technique, use it in a rough draft and ask your professor.

The Beginning: The Introductory Paragraph

Also called the *introduction* for good reason, your beginning or first paragraph initiates your relationship with your readers. You *introduce* yourself to your audience by your breadth of knowledge, ability to communicate effectively, and command of tone and purpose. You also *introduce* or acquaint your audience to the subject matter. As the author, you come to the piece with more knowledge than your readers, especially if you have conducted research, so your central job with the beginning involves quickly catching your readers up to speed. Therefore, an introduction might include:

- Definition of initial terms
- Brief history of the issue
- Any controversies
- The main players and their credentials
- The thesis statement

When writing an introduction, remember that first impressions are lasting ones. Studies about how people read reveal that test subjects read first and last paragraphs much more closely than the rest of a piece, so use your first paragraph to "hook" your audience. As you learned in *The Thomson Reader,* "sparking" your readers' interests can be achieved by using several techniques.

The Startle or Shock Strategy

Snap your readers to attention by opening with an amazing, shocking, or even controversial scenario or sentence.

If you are reading this, then the world was spared the most horrific meteor collision in its history.

So there really might be little green men in outer space and we are not alone, according to scientific data beamed back from NASA's *Voyager.*

The Balanced Approach

Establish goodwill and ethos (credibility) with your audience by presenting multiple points about an issue before revealing yours through your thesis.

Much controversy surrounds the use of the National Sex Offender Registry. Many citizens and law enforcement agencies believe the public has the right to know whether a convicted sex offender is living or working in their neighborhoods. However, others believe that access to such information violates individual rights for our citizens. By carefully examining the National Sex Offender Public Registry, maintained by the Office of the Attorney General, and data from interviews and newspaper articles, the choice to register as many known sex offender felons as possible should be easy to affirm.

Lead with a Quotation

Often a famous or pertinent quotation captures the essence of your subject matter perfectly.

> "Getting old ain't for sissies," famously observed Betty Davis, and now I understand why.

Define Your Terms

When employing specialized terms or ones you are not sure your audience will recognize, use the first paragraph to familiarize readers. However, avoid using a dictionary or encyclopedia, which limits the scope of your investigation.

> The sugar glider is a tree-dwelling marsupial found in Australia and India. They are very social animals, preferring to live in groups or packs ranging from 20–50, and have been domesticated as pets recently.

Anecdotal Information or Dialogue

Instead of an imaginary scenario, try leading off with actual dialogue or an anecdote that describes the issue you plan to discuss.

> Me: Which game do you want to play, little brother?
>
> Jay: *Candyland*!
>
> Me: What a surprise. We played that yesterday. Don't you want to try another?
>
> Jay: *Candyland*!
>
> Who knew back in 1949 when a woman from San Diego sold her invention called *Candyland* to Milton Bradley Toys, that she was selling one of the world's most popular games for children?

The Rhetorical Question

When authors write a rhetorical question they do not expect an answer; rather, this technique is designed to raise questions and issues that the author plans to address and that readers might not have thought of. This is a good introductory strategy, but writers tend to overuse it.

> Who could have known the disaster that would occur on September 11, 2001? Certainly not any of the victims as they dressed for work, meetings, a trip to New York, a flight to Los Angeles, an interview in the Pentagon, and all the other tasks that would never be completed.

The Middle or the Body

Like your introduction and your conclusion, the paragraphs that form the **body** of your essay have specific duties, namely they support and provide the detailed explanations for your thesis. Therefore, after setting up the introduction, think of the **thesis** as a segue or natural transition into the actual discussion or body, so that your paper begins by acquainting your readers with the material, gives an explicit roadmap to the rest of the paper, and, by the second or third paragraph, launches into the support and thesis-defining material.

Dividing your paper into chunks of specific duties creates a structure that looks like this:

Definition of initial terms
Brief history of the issue
Any controversies   Introductory Paragraph
The main players and their credentials
The thesis statement

Topic sentence
Support for Thesis Point 1   Body Paragraph 1

Topic sentence
Support for Thesis Point 2   Body Paragraph 2

Topic sentence
Support for Thesis Point 3   Body Paragraph 3

Topic sentence
Support for Thesis Point 4   Body Paragraph 4

Wrap up all issues
Restate thesis   Conclusion
Conclude with a purpose
Final remarks for readers

Works Cited

Amichai, Yehuda. "Jews in the Land of Israel." <u>The Selected Poetry of Yehuda Amichai</u>.
    Ed. and Trans. Chana Bloch and Stephen Mitchell. Berkeley: University of California
    Press, 1996.

Darwish, Mahmoud. "Excerpts from the Byzantine Odes of Abu Firas." <u>Unfortunately,
    It Was Paradise: Selected Poems</u>. Ed. and Trans. Munir Akash, Sinan Antoon, Amira
    El-Zein, and Carolyn Forche. Berkeley: University of California Press, 2003.

The main concern when crafting the body section of your paper should be about flow. That is, do the paragraphs follow an easy order? Flow and order are dictated by your thesis statement and the type of paper you are writing.

Given the following thesis statement:

In May, Sedona, Arizona, is an excellent tourist destination because the weather is mild, the desert vegetation is at its peak, there are many outdoor art exhibits to tour, local animals are more active, and the tourist season is still a month away.

The paper should look like this:

Introduction

Body Paragraph 1: discusses Sedona's mild weather in March

Body Paragraph 2: discusses the peak desert vegetation

Body Paragraph 3: discusses the many outdoor art shows

Body Paragraph 4: discusses the activity of the local animals

Body Paragraph 5: discusses how the tourist season is a month away

Conclusion: reminds readers of the reasons why we should go to Sedona, Arizona, in March.

However, in looking at the chart, some of the paragraphs can be moved around for better sense. For example, the fact that the desert vegetation and its animal population are at their best during this time indicates these two paragraphs are similar enough that they should be together. Also, the weather is probably a factor contributing to the popularity of outdoor art shows, making those two paragraphs naturally connected.

A revised chart might look like this:

Introduction

Body Paragraph 1: discusses Sedona's mild weather in March

Body Paragraph 2: discusses the many outdoor art shows

Body Paragraph 3: discusses the peak desert vegetation

Body Paragraph 4: discusses the activity of the local animals

Body Paragraph 5: discusses how the tourist season is a month away

Conclusion: reminds readers of the reasons why we should go to Sedona, Arizona, in March.

The type of assignment also dictates the order in which you structure your paragraphs. For example, **narratives** often follow chronological order; **comparison and contrast** papers cover one side and then the other side; **process** essays follow a rigid order dictated by steps; and a research paper can apply almost any form the author chooses.

Another governing principle for your paper's structure is whether you begin with **specific** data and end with more **general** information or start with **general** information and end with the **specific** data.

Most writers choose to start with general information and build to a specific conclusion. For example:

The NBA's road to the final four involves a lengthy season of games that leads to playoffs and finally a championship.

From this sentence we can assume that the author will cover in a chronological fashion the National Basketball Association's season, from the broad beginning where all teams are contenders to culminate in a championship playoff between two teams.

The same writer could choose to move from the specific to the general by beginning with the events of the playoff and concluding with the general information about the start of the season.

> The excitement of the NBA final championship capped off an unusually boring season this year.

Conclusion Techniques

Unless you are asked to write narratives or memoirs, most of your college writing assignments provide no reason for you to personally interact with your audience. However, the introduction and conclusion sections of your essays are the most opportune places to relate to your readers and convey to them your position and the strategies you will engage during the paper.

The **conclusion paragraph** provides your readers with a lasting impression. Whatever you have said or done in the paper will be memorable, but the conclusion controls the essay with the last word.

Concluding paragraphs should:

- reaffirm the thesis
- establish a rapport or relationship with readers and remind them how they have evolved and grown in their knowledge from the beginning of the paper to the end
- review the issues and positions covered in the paper
- leave a memorable impression

Strategies

Much like the introduction, writers see conclusions as opportunities to exercise some creativity. In many cases, authors remain behind the work and out of the way until the conclusion, where they employ tone and language to convey strong and active opinions.

> In short, this despicable problem with the maltreatment of homeless people in the neighborhood must be resolved quickly. (*Strong language demonstrates the author's stand whereas throughout the paper the author may have remained neutral.*)

Ask the audience to become involved or delve further:

> Learn more about the benefits of sustainable farming by researching local participating farms and businesses. (*Now that you've read my paper, join me.*)

Encourage your audience to take action:

> Clearly, the ongoing crime reports regarding the maltreatment of homeless people must become first page news in order for all parties to be satisfied. Cast your November 4th vote for the amendment. (*Do something to show your support.*)

Remind the audience of the important elements discussed throughout the essay:

> To recap the critical issues affecting the homeless population and the local community, there are two opposing factions with equally strong opinions. (*Certain issues must not get lost in the conclusion.*)

Leave your audience with a rhetorical question:

> If the sheriff's office has done nothing wrong, why are they not returning the newspaper's phone requests for interviews? *(In case you missed this point, let me lead you to the important issue you should ponder.)*

The conclusion should not introduce material not presented in the paper:

> An entirely new issue to the controversy is whether the school board knew the new staff members had not been subjected to a background clearance check. *(Your job is not to continue educating or informing your readers on matters outside of the paper.)*

Conclusion Checklist:

How does the conclusion demonstrate the importance of the thesis?

Does the conclusion touch upon the evidence from the paper?

Does the conclusion establish a relationship with your readers?

Do you ask your readers to become involved or active with your issue?

Do you resolve all problems and topics discussed in the paper?

Do you introduce new material not presented in the paper?

Technology Toolbox

Using the Comment Feature

Your word processor's "Comment" feature allows you many opportunities to respond to your own paper or to a peer's paper. When you choose "Comment" a small red bar appears to far right with an oblong balloon ready to accept your remarks. Use this feature to remind yourself to insert source material, or to find a quotation or example to support your claim. When reading a friend's paper you can ask questions and make suggestions. All authors have the option to delete the comments later during revision, so nothing is permanent.

Level 1

Name _____ **Date** _____

DIRECTIONS List the information you believe should be included in an introductory paragraph for each of the topics below.

SAMPLE

Topic: Culture in New Orleans

New Orleans is a region different from any other in the U.S. Define creole and how that creates a unique atmosphere, discuss the origins of New Orleans jazz, food specific to the region, and the French Quarter.

1. Topic: Registering for classes

   _____

   _____

2. Topic: The perils of online shopping

   _____

   _____

3. Topic: Should college athletes get paid?

   _____

   _____

4. Topic: How to be a good student

   _____

   _____

5. Topic: Halloween is an important holiday

   _____

   _____

6. Topic: Protecting the First Amendment

_____

_____

Level 1

Name_____ **Date**_____

DIRECTIONS Use the following information below, but rewrite the material in your own words to reflect your purpose and to create an introductory paragraph by applying the various introductory strategies from this chapter and *The Thomson Handbook*.

Playing board games has entertained families and friends for decades. Children learn how to observe rules, count, recognize opportunities for reward, and also about consequences from games like *Candyland*. Some enjoy games with more strategy like *Risk* and *Battleship*. *Life* and *Monopoly* encourage fiscal responsibility, and *Pictionary* and *Cranium* require creativity. Most believe games create a sense of competition.

Startle or Shock Introduction:

_____

_____

_____

Balanced Introduction:

_____

_____

_____

Quotation Introduction:

_____

_____

_____

Definition Introduction:

_____

_____

_____

Rhetorical Question Introduction:

_____

_____

_____

Anecdotal Introduction:

_____

_____

_____

Which of the various techniques did you think most effectively worked with the topic and why?

_____

_____

_____

Level 1

Name_____ Date_____

DIRECTIONS The information in the following paragraphs is mixed up and out of order. Using the lines provided, revise the paragraphs to list the best possible structure.

1. Land and water animals make estuaries their homes. Estuaries are mixtures of fresh and salt water. They are subject to tides. These areas are critical to environmental health. Except for deep sea fish, most fishermen make their livings in the estuaries. These areas can be called wetlands, lagoons, sounds, inlets, or creeks. Animal life is so abundant and dependent on estuary conditions to survive that these areas have been called "the nurseries of the sea." Estuaries are the buffer zones between large bodies of water like oceans and the land.

   _____

   _____

   _____

2. It rains in Seattle, Washington about 50% of the time. The city was named after Chief Sealth, leader of the Suquamish Indians. One of the fittest cities in the nation, Seattle has many organized trails for walkers, runners, and bikers. People can take a short ferry ride to Sidney, British Colombia. Home to a thriving arts culture, Seattle has about 30 museums and galleries.

   _____

   _____

   _____

Level 2

Name_____ **Date**_____

DIRECTIONS Read Kristin's essay in Chapter 16 and rewrite her conclusion using the prompts below.

1. Ask the audience to become involved or delve further.

_____

_____

_____

2. Remind the audience of the important elements discussed throughout the essay.

_____

_____

_____

3. Leave your audience with a rhetorical question.

_____

_____

_____

4. Encourage your audience to take action.

_____

_____

_____

bread and the research you have gathered is the sandwich fixings snugly located between the pieces of bread.

Each time you utilize one of your outside sources you must provide an introduction to demonstrate context, relevance, and your thoughts

Plus

outside material to support your thoughts

Plus

a conclusion to reaffirm context, relevance, your thoughts, and to transition to the next point.

You	Other author	You
Introduction	Outside Source	Wrap Up

In the following example a student creates a sandwich in her biodiversity paper. Her voice is bolded.

Danielle Brigida
BIO 202

Coral Reef Bleaching: A Threat to the Earth's Biodiversity

Within the past few decades, vast quantities of coral have been lost due to a reaction called bleaching. Many government agencies all over the world are taking an interest in the health of coral reefs. The EPA web site claims, "These measures may include actions to address problems such as land-based sources of water pollution. . ." **By learning more about the reefs and what is necessary to keep them as stable ecosystems, nations all over the world are becoming more aware of ways to protect reefs and prevent bleaching.**

Danielle states the problem and then demonstrates that her goal in presenting the information on the Environmental Protection Agency's Web site is to support her idea that governments recognize they must participate in maintaining coral reef health. She keeps her voice *dominant* in the paragraph so the outside source does not become overbearing or drown hers out while *blending* her ideas with those from an outside source. If she did not adopt this strategy, the quoted material would have no context and would appear out of place in the paper.

Your commentary becomes the difference between **reporting** and **analyzing** information.

Abrupt and choppy quotation:

Kristin Brickley
English 203

Lau Po teaches Waverly "The Double Attack from the East and West Shores" and "Sand in the Eyes of Advancing Forces" (Tan 646). Waverly learned "A little knowledge withheld is a great advantage one should store for future use . . . one must show and never tell" (Tan 646).

Well-blended quotation:
This gentleman, Lau Po, teaches Waverly **of the chess strategies that he knows with names such as** "The Double Attack from the East and West Shores" and "Sand in the Eyes of Advancing Forces" (Tan 646). Waverly, **being an attentive pupil,** learned **all of these strategies and even formulates one of her own:** "A little knowledge withheld is a great advantage one should store for future use . . . one must show and never tell" (Tan 646). **This is a pivotal realization for Waverly in her endeavors not only to play chess and win tournaments, but to learn about her own invisible strength.**

In the first example, there is too little contextual explanation, so the reader cannot determine how well Kristin understands the strategies she describes or if she is merely reporting.

Varying the Blending Language

Once you begin habitually introducing and concluding outside source materials in the sandwich method, you will probably find you need to remind yourself to vary your language to avoid simplistic and repetitive phrases. For example, many writers use "said" to introduce quoted material.

> Ms. Todesco **said,** "Flying into Boston and renting a car is your best option."

> The paper **said** today was going to be hot.

> "I did not know those contributions were illegal," **said** the senator.

The same sentences with more creative language convey greater intensity.

> Ms. Todesco **helpfully explained,** "Flying into Boston and renting a car is your best option."

> The paper **warned its readers that** today was going to be hot.

> **When faced with a mob of reporters, the senator growled,** "I did not know those contributions were illegal."

Your language choices signal emotion, opinion, and relationships between yourself and your sources, as well as relationships between your sources. While the parties may agree on some points, many will have divergent thoughts and you must faithfully replicate these elements.

> The city council vehemently opposes the Talbot Park Civic League's proposal to ban on-street parking near the high school, according to a source close to a council member.

> Although the civic league is hopeful, a source within the council's office confirmed the council will not vote on the measure.

> One issue both the civic league and the council agree upon is the rezoning plan for new condominiums.

A Partial List of "Says" Substitutions

acknowledges	denies	growls	screams
affirms	disagrees (with)	indicates	suggests
believes	discusses	jokes	supports
claims	echoes	observes	
concludes	feels	repeats	
confirms	finds	reports	

Summarizing

When reading articles and book chapters to prepare to write your paper, you will need to **summarize** or condense many pages of material into a few sentences. To do so you must learn what is relevant and what is extraneous to your audience's ability to understand your meaning. A summary also faithfully replicates the original in its order and meaning, so when determining what stays and what you cut, make sure to follow the author's original plan and create a shortened version without examples, charts, visuals, and other strategies.

Original:

Kristin Brickley
4/20/06

"Victims of Circumstance"

Ireland has admittedly faced a tremulous history. Throughout Irish history, social and political uprisings are more prevalent than eras of peace and prosperity. The twentieth century also brought conflict with the Easter Rising in 1916 and then the Anglo-Irish War. These years of growing pains were certainly difficult for the Irish but they also performed the important function of shaping a strong and resilient Irish people. However, years of strife also created a sense of stasis in the country and a widely held belief that victimization had created circumstances that were beyond human control. The theater and literature of the 20th century document this stasis and victimization as the country continued to work through its growing pains.

Poor summary:

Ireland has had a tumultuous history with numerous social and political uprisings and less eras of peace and prosperity. However difficult the bad times, they helped shape the Irish of today into a determined people. Unfortunately, the years of strife made the people feel victimized beyond their control. (Though condensed enough, too much of the author's original wording appears without proper quotation.)

Appropriate summary:

Ireland has had a tumultuous history marked by more cultural and political trouble than good times of positive growth. These unfortunate times have simultaneously created a tough and determined population that remains vulnerable to issues they cannot possibly manage.

Direct Quotations and Paraphrases

When replicating someone else's ideas, writers basically have two choices: to directly quote the source or to reword that source in their own words.

When you quote someone else's words or speech, you must record precisely the original text and punctuation, even if the original contains errors, and all within double quotation marks. If you do not clearly indicate someone else's work with quotation marks, you are plagiarizing. Additionally, you must always provide the source material in parentheses immediately after the quoted or paraphrased material. This is called a **parenthetical source citation** and is discussed at length in the end of this chapter. Failure to provide this important element results in plagiarism.

Original text:

"Maureen in The Beauty Queen of Leenane, and Bridie in The Ballroom of Romance, each believes that their fate is all but decided by the circumstances that are created by their victimization" (Brickley 5).

Plagiarized text:

Kristin Brickley observes that Maureen in The Beauty Queen of Leenane, and Bridie in The Ballroom of Romance have had their fate all but decided by the circumstances that are created by their victimization. *(Some wording has been changed and the piece lacks quotation marks)*

Plagiarized text:

Kristin Brickley observes that "Maureen in <u>The Beauty Queen of Leenane,</u> and Bridie in <u>The Ballroom of Romance</u> have had their fate all but decided by the circumstances that are created by their victimization." (Some wording has been changed and there is no parenthetical citation to attribute to the author.)

Use direct quotations sparingly, and always try to paraphrase the material. Too much quoted material threatens the authenticity of your work, distracts readers from your message, and changes the tone from your voice to the quoted voice.

Use quotations to:

■ Capture a thought that has been so well expressed or done with such remarkable language that you could not possibly do justice with paraphrasing. Example: Franklin Roosevelt's "The only thing we have to fear is fear itself."

■ Replicate the essence when paraphrasing would lengthen or make awkward the original text.

For a list of more instances when quotations are acceptable, consult *The Thomson Handbook*, Chapter 17, page 346.

How to Punctuate a Quotation

Any word or phrase you are quoting directly must appear in double quotation marks (" ") and if the quotation contains a quotation, the one within must appear in single quotation marks (' '). The sentence's end punctuation, usually a period, goes on the outside of the **parenthetical source citation,** which is usually the author's last name and the page number where the original material may be found. For example, (Brickley 5) tells us that the author's last name is Brickley and the material is located on page 5 of the text.

Paraphrasing

Whereas a summary is a condensed version of a source that is meant to convey the central issue or idea, a **paraphrase** provides as much detail as the original source but it is interpreted by you and then restated in your own words. Like the summary, when you paraphrase you must replicate the original author's sequence of events, the tone and attitude, and meaning. Also like the summary, you may not include your ideas or opinions until you finish paraphrasing because your readers need to be able to distinguish your ideas from those of the original author.

You will want to paraphrase most of the outside material you use in research because paraphrasing creates a stronger paper than one filled with copied quotations.

Original passage:

"Similar to that of most young boys during the late 16th century, William Shakespeare had been raised a disciplined student of Renaissance learning. Exposed to the revived works of such ancient Roman authors as Ovid and Virgil, the young Elizabethan had undoubtedly been given a profound education in some of history's oldest and most renowned literary heroes" (Hilleary 1).

Paraphrased:

According to Mike Hilleary, much like his contemporaries, 16th century playwright William Shakespeare was a product of the Renaissance education. As such, he must have been intimately familiar with the classical Roman authors Ovid and Virgil and probably possessed an impressive knowledge of other famous literary authors and their characters (1). (The paraphrased version credits student author in the beginning, follows his attitude and central idea, and gives proper parenthetical citation at the end of the passage.)

Original passage:
"But just as the instruction in these particular texts would inevitably enable him to construct his own kind of heroic characters—as he would mature and turn to the profession of a playwright—it would consequently provide him with the additional knowledge for creating one of literature's greatest villains" (Hilleary 1).

Paraphrased:
By extension, as he aged Shakespeare's education in the classics combined with his maturation enabled the famous playwright to create one of the finest anti-heroes in literature (Hilleary 1).

Parenthetical and In-Text Source Citations

To avoid even the appearance of **plagiarism,** or passing someone else's work off as your own, whether deliberate or accidental, make sure you accurately credit the work you use to inform your own ideas in papers.

Two ways of making sure you account for the work of other people are to use **parenthetical source citations,** which are the author's last name and the page number from the original source of the information, and **in-text source citations,** which credit the author in the sentence. Regardless of whether you do or do not use the in-text method, **you must always parenthetically cite anyone else's ideas, whether direct quotes or paraphrased.**

Parenthetical Sources

Parenthetical information consists of the author's last name, if given in the original source, and the page number: "Throughout Shakespeare's works, the soliloquy was a standard method by means of which the audience might come to know a character's private thoughts" (Hilleary 5). From this we know we can go to page 5 in Mike Hilleary's paper and find this exact passage.

If you include the author in your sentence, omit the last name from the parenthetical citation:

According to Mike Hilleary, "throughout Shakespeare's works, the soliloquy was a standard method by means of which the audience might come to know a character's private thoughts" (5).

In cases where no author has been listed, use the first key word in the title:

The author pretends to ignore the historical influences of the day and their effect on Shakespeare (Discussion 45).

When an online source does not provide page numbers, you must provide the title and author in your sentence:

On her Web site about the Masaai Organization, author Chvonne Parker explains how the Masaai people need international help and relief.

For a more extensive treatment of source citations in the various documentation styles, consult *The Thomson Handbook*, Chapters 19–22.

Level 1

Name_____ **Date**_____

DIRECTIONS Following are some quotations that need to be introduced and concluded. Write sentences for the "bread" for these "sandwich fixings." Use your imagination to determine the missing context.

SAMPLE

"Many police officers do not like to respond to domestic abuse calls."

Issues involving domestic abuse have become a giant drain on the local law enforcement. A department source recently revealed, "Many police officers do not like to respond to domestic abuse calls." No doubt the officers dread the instability they find at the scene when one or both parties are high on alcohol or drugs.

1. "The airline has recently undergone financial problems but hopes to keep its workers from striking."

   _____

   _____

2. "A diet high in fruits and vegetables greatly reduces the chances for health problems in later years."

   _____

   _____

3. "Consumers must understand the inherent risks involved in online shopping."

   _____

   _____

4. "The American Dental Society recommends a daily regime of flossing and brushing to prevent tooth decay."

   _____

   _____

5. "Nevada's National Guard has been dispatched to some of the wildfire locations."

_____

_____

6. "The child apparently got lost in the woods while on a picnic with her family."

_____

_____

Level 1

Name _____ **Date** _____

DIRECTIONS Revise the following quotations and paraphrases to vary the language. Use your imagination to provide context and circumstances.

SAMPLE

The unidentified woman said, "I am not trying to cause trouble."

The unidentified woman pacing in front of the store in a dirty hospital gown shrieked, "I am not trying to cause trouble."

1. After working in the heat at his construction job Jamie came home and said, "I am looking for a new job."

    _____

    _____

2. Kate and Bridget said, "We did not play that practical joke on our suitemates. It must have been someone else."

    _____

    _____

3. When Jennifer called in sick she said, "I have been up all night with a fever and a sore throat."

    _____

    _____

4. Lizzie said, "I'll watch the kids" after seeing no one else volunteer.

    _____

    _____

5. The reporter pulled me aside and said, "You should stick around because the Congressman is about to say something very important."

    _____

    _____

6. "News of my death has been greatly exaggerated," said the swimmer after being rescued from the waterfalls.

_____

_____

7. Although the president is not optimistic about the war, he said, "We must stay the course."

_____

_____

Level 1

Name_____ **Date**_____

DIRECTIONS Summarize the following passages written by students Boone Brousseau and Danielle Brigida using the rules you have learned in this chapter and in Chapter 17 of *The Thomson Handbook.*

1. "People all over the world tend to think the conflict in Iraq is hopeless and will end in a bitter civil war, destroying the country and the people that occupy it. Iraq is not hopeless though, it is merely frustrated. Iraq will find the peace and freedom that it has dreamed of for so long, primarily because of the hope that is left in the youth, culture, and countries like America that are helping fight for it" (Brousseau 1).

   _____

   _____

2. "The book discusses how globalization is threatening the world on environmental, economical, and ethical levels. Readers learn about the overwhelming downsides that the globalization era has elicited. While globalization has expanded the wealth of a few hundred corporations, a majority of people in most parts of the world are suffering" (Brigida 1).

   _____

   _____

3. "In our environmental conservation class we have covered everything from the poverty in underdeveloped countries and population problems to the awful degradation of forests and the mistreatment of soils. This book takes a closer look at some of the solutions concerning the economic and environmental changes that need to be made in order to make earth a sustainable living place" (Brigida 1).

   _____

   _____

4. "Iraq has a bright future ahead of it. The hopelessness that is felt by so many is merely misinterpreted frustration. In time, the problems of Iraq will be solved and the needs will be filled. The youth, though living in a land of terror and war, have too much hope to give up. The culture of the Iraqi people, though struggling in a land seemingly void of passion and beauty will survive and adapt. American troops,

though homesick and tired, will continue to train as long as hope remains"
(Brousseau 4).

_____

_____

Level 1

Name_____ Date_____

DIRECTIONS Paraphrase the following passages written by student writer Mike Hilleary.

1. "In 1604 Elizabethan playwright William Shakespeare constructed a play about a black soldier named Othello who is wrongfully manipulated into believing that his wife is having an affair with another man" (Hilleary 9).

_____

_____

2. "Throughout Shakespeare's works, the soliloquy was a standard method by means of which the audience might come to know a character's private thoughts" (Hilleary 5).

_____

_____

3. "If an injured Iago were given due cause for his vengeance, one would feel as an audience member a certain inclination to respond with some form of sympathy. However, due to certain actions throughout the play, such sympathy proves quite difficult to develop" (Hilleary 8).

_____

_____

4. "For many contemporary critics the majority of Iago's motivation stems not from some social expectation to act against infidelity, but rather from his inability to control his own inner emotional jealousy towards the greater fortunes of those around him" (Hilleary 8).

_____

_____

5. "Whether it is because of his own constitutional conditions or because the experience of it had never existed in a consistent way throughout his life, Iago's mindset is unable to identify with the qualities of what is good" (Hilleary 9).

_____

_____

Level 1

Name_____ **Date**_____

DIRECTIONS Rewrite each of the following quotations by paraphrasing the information and include the author's name and/or title of the article in the sentence.

SAMPLE

"The future of the common tree frog is unclear at this point due to deforestation and loss of its natural habitat." Dr. Emma Peele

Dr. Emma Peele's research leads her to believe that problems with the environment are jeopardizing the future of the common tree frog.

1. "Character cannot be developed in ease and quiet. Only through experience of trial and suffering can the soul be strengthened, ambition inspired and success achieved." Helen Keller

   _____

   _____

2. "Always acknowledge a fault. This will throw those in power off their guard and give you an opportunity to commit more." Mark Twain

   _____

   _____

3. "I can win any argument on any topic against any opponent. People know this, and steer clear of me at parties. Often, as a sign of great respect, they don't even invite me." Dave Barry

   _____

   _____

4. "Getting my lifelong weight struggle under control has come from a process of treating myself as well as I treat others in every way." Oprah Winfrey

   _____

   _____

5. "I think it is the duty of the comedian to find out where the line is drawn and cross that line deliberately." George Carlin

_____

_____

Level 1

Name _____ **Date** _____

DIRECTIONS Experiment with your authentic voice by paraphrasing the quotations below and including several lines of your own commentary. Each of the prompts provides the style of tone and voice you should use.

1. "After much debate in the scientific community, it seems as though global warming is a very real reality and danger," expressed scientist Cynthia Adkins.

   _____

   _____

2. "I faced the corporate glass ceiling and I smashed it to bits," grinned business mogul Jane Kabana.

   _____

   _____

3. "We have caught the congressman with his hand in the cookie jar. Now we must figure out how to try him for embezzlement," announced attorney Suzy Phillips.

   _____

   _____

4. "Regardless of what you may have been told, being a working mother means working two jobs," claims working mother Debbie East.

   _____

   _____

5. "Working as an ultrasound technician means I am helping people live longer by combating their illnesses," explained Janet Puzz.

   _____

   _____

Level 2

Name_____ **Date**_____

DIRECTIONS Choose two topics from the following list or one you plan to research for class (clear this with your professor first). Then create two complete "research packages" in which you identify:

- the most suitable audience and justify why it is the most suitable
- a focused purpose for writing the paper to that audience where you establish the significance and importance of the problem and how it affects the audience
- a research question to pose and answer
- the appropriate language and tone choice
- a sample thesis

Topic List

Protecting an endangered species
Alternatives to oil-based fuel
Same-sex universities
Mandatory laptops for incoming freshmen

Topic:

Audience and Why Best Suited:

Focused Purpose:

Significance/Importance of Problem to Audience:

Research Question and Answer:

Appropriate Language/Tone/Style:

Sample Thesis:

Topic:

Audience and Why Best Suited:

Focused Purpose:

Significance/Importance of Problem to Audience:

Research Question and Answer:

Appropriate Language/Tone/Style:

Sample Thesis:

Revision Strategies

The Thomson Handbook, **Chapter 6**

On page 87 of *The Thomson Handbook* you read that "Revision is an act of discovery." Why *discovery* when you have already written the paper, you ask? Because each time we *re*vise, *re*visit, and *re*member what we have written we write with greater clarity, create crisper sentences, and find more appropriate order. Essentially, we discover more interesting ways of expressing ourselves than we previously understood.

Revision is the most critically important component of your writing process because, as writers on all levels have long understood, the difference between a mediocre writer and a good one is the level of revision we are willing to commit. Most authors say revision takes two to three times longer than the drafting process, and many are still not satisfied with their final, printed results.

Revision means tearing apart sentences, throwing out unusable paragraphs, rewriting introductions and conclusions, and making a wonderful mess out of the neatly typed first draft. Some hesitate at first, trying to believe their first effort is the best, but once you take the plunge, your writing and your grades will improve dramatically.

Pulitzer Prize-winning author Toni Morrison believes so strongly in the power of revision that the themes in her books center on revisiting, remembering, and revising.

Prolific author Stephen King compares writing to carpentry, a skill that must be perpetually reworked and revised in order to produce the desired effect.

Poet Walt Whitman was not content with his epic *Leaves of Grass,* to the point that he revised the book nine times over 37 years!

As Chapter 6 in *The Thomson Handbook* explains, revision work can apply to many different elements in your writing, such as whether you chose an audience and addressed them appropriately, whether your purpose is clearly defined and available, and kairos, or whether the project is timely.

When completing the exercises in this chapter, you should refer to the Project Checklists in *The Thomson Handbook* located on pages 90, 94, 95, as well as Activity 6.6, and the Paramedic Method.

Whether you adopt the practices in *The Thomson Handbook, The Thomson Handbook Workbook,* or create a unique combination that involves both and a bit of your own style, remember that revision is much more than checking for grammar, spelling errors, and changing a couple of words or sentences.

Revision is chaotic, often messy, but very rewarding!

The revision process occurs on these levels:

- Language (verbs, descriptions)
- Sentence (length, cadence)

- Paragraph (order, sequence)
- Grammatical (editing)

The Language Revision Process

In this stage of the writing process you should rewrite on both sentence and paragraph levels to consider your **audience, word choice and variety, clarity, purpose, tone, evidence,** and **visual content.**

Questions to ask when revising for audience:

- Who is my audience?
- Is there a more appropriate audience for this subject?
- Where in the paper do I make sure to appeal to them? (Go through your paper and write *audience* in every instance you find where you explicitly and implicitly consider them.)
- Where in the paper can I add more to appeal to my audience's logic, ethics, and emotion?

Example:

Audience: Freshman Class

    Stem cell research is a controversial issue that is currently being discussed in places from the White House to our parents' houses. Recent surveys show that most Americans overwhelmingly favor stem cell research, but the president disagrees. Unfortunately, part of the problem is in how the stem cells are procured. Those in favor of the research want the stem cells that have already been extracted under different medical procedures to be used, whereas opponents think the stem cells in question have yet to be harvested.

Problem:

This paragraph makes only one attempt to identify with its intended audience in the first line. Also, how is the freshman class the most appropriate audience? In rereading this, perhaps this should be revised to appeal to the Senate. That way the paragraph could include information about the discrepancy between the will of the people and how the Senate's job is to represent their constituents to appeal to their sense of ethical responsibility and emotion.

Revision:

Audience: The Senate

    Recently members of the Senate have found themselves in a watershed moment where they can actually conduct the work of the people who voted them into office and whose needs they must faithfully heed, or turn their backs on their constituents and vote against an urgent bill. This issue involves stem cell research, and if any group can positively affect the history and health of the American nation, the leaders in the United States Senate are the ones. Stand up for this important bill, make sure the most up-to-date and correct information is being presented to the American public, and vote for stem cell research so that the citizens of this country will get the opportunity for excellent health care.

Questions to ask when revising for word choice and variety:

- Do I repeat myself or certain words or phrases? (If you revise on your computer, use the "Find" function to see how often you repeat key words and phrases.)
- Where are my "to be" verbs and how do I revise using stronger verb choices?
- In general, how can I heighten the level of comprehension by revising my word choice to include a greater variety of terms?
- Which terms can I substitute with words from my thesaurus?

Example:

Football fans in Tallahassee are all about football games, read about football in the papers and books, put football paraphernalia on their cars, and wear football jerseys. This is known as suffering from Football Hysteria, a condition where people become obsessed with Florida State football to the point that they check out of their lives. Many have started going to a therapist for advice on how to stop attending football games, stop watching football on television, and not wearing or advertising football teams or players.

Problem:

The word *football* is repeated to the point that the piece is annoyingly repetitious. The author's verbs are repetitively "to be" verbs that do not provide strength and the sentences reveal the author relies on very general word choices and slang expressions that could easily be beefed up with revision and sentence combinations.

Revision:

Fans in Tallahassee bear a long history of fanatical support for Florida State University's nationally ranked football team. Experts call this condition Football Hysteria which affects those obsessed with the team to the point that they cannot function properly. Many have sought therapy to help control their urgings and the disorder, and experts suggest affected people should cease attending games or watching the sport on television and refuse to adorn their cars and bodies with paraphernalia.

Questions to ask when revising for clarity:

- Have I properly defined all key terms?
- If someone other than I read this paper, would he or she understand my meaning?
- What areas are vague or less than specific?
- Have I used *it* to express my meaning? (Use the "Find" function to search for how many times you use *it* improperly.)

Example:

If someone is convicted of vehicular manslaughter it can be a felony or a misdemeanor, and both require jail time. The problem is when trying to decide if the person deliberately did it or did not mean to do it, and it is difficult to decide if the person was premeditating or didn't plan anything. Lawmakers, lawyers, and judges are not doing enough to make this terrible issue important, and they are responsible for our welfare, so they should have to get tough.

Problem:

Without having been provided a definition for *vehicular manslaughter, felony,* and *misdemeanor,* the audience has little clue about the purpose of the paragraph. Too much reliance on *it,* and other vague terms like *this, anything,* and *enough* further confuse the reader.

Revision:

A person can be convicted of vehicular manslaughter if he or she willfully or deliberately kills someone while driving drunk or grossly negligent. For example, if a person loses control and wrecks the car while speeding and kills a passenger, he or she has committed vehicular manslaughter. Depending on the circumstances, such as if the event was planned or premeditated, this crime can be categorized as either a felony, punishable by mandatory jail time, or a misdemeanor, a lesser offense that can be satisfied by a short jail sentence in a local jail or fine. Because more innocent people lose their lives to vehicular manslaughter, lawmakers must pass more stringent laws to discourage offenders.

Questions to ask when revising for tone:

- What was my attitude about the subject and the audience?
- Where is that attitude strongest and weakest in the paper?
- How can I strengthen the tone I use to heighten my voice and opinion?
- Have I given enough consideration for an audience who disagrees with my thesis and support?
- Are there any places in the paper where my tone becomes inconsistent or confusing?

Example:

If someone drives drunk and kills someone, that person should have to pay for the rest of his or her rotten life. There is no excuse for driving after getting drunk except stupidity. Too many innocent adults and children have died at the hands of a selfish moron who does not have enough sense to quit drinking or get a ride instead of climbing behind the wheel of a loaded weapon.

Problem:

The author's contemptuous attitude distracts from any worthwhile comments because the reader cannot see beyond the emotional language. This kind of overwhelmingly hostile tone will put off even readers who would normally agree with the material.

Revision:

Too many drunken drivers get a light slap on the wrist after killing and hurting innocent victims; therefore, legislators must increase laws to prosecute even first-time offenders. Unlike a typical driving accident, driving while intoxicated is a crime that is easily avoided with acting responsibly. Stricter laws will discourage drunks from climbing behind the wheel of a lethal weapon and ruining other people's lives.

Questions to ask when revising for evidence:

- Where are the areas in which I forget to provide evidence to support my opinions or claims?
- What evidence can create an even stronger case for my claims and support?
- Have I varied and mingled the different outside sources?

Example:

Benjamin Franklin taught readers in a humorous and entertaining way in the greater Philadelphia area on a number of issues. For example, he explains in one "Maxim" how people should keep their visits short so their hosts do not have to figure out how to get rid of them. He also calls people who go to the doctor too much "fools."

Problem:

Since this information is too detailed to be part of the greater body of public knowledge, this passage must have source citations to demonstrate its authenticity and that there is no plagiarism.

Revision:

In his famous *Poor Richard's Almanack* (1733–1758) Benjamin Franklin taught readers in a humorous and entertaining way in the greater Philadelphia area on a number of issues. For example, he explains in his first "Maxim" how people should keep their visits short so their hosts do not have to figure out how to get rid of them (Franklin 3). He also calls people who go to the doctor too much "fools" (Franklin 4).

Editing Grammar and Mechanics

Though it is tempting to revise along the way, resist the impulse to even correct a spelling error in your first draft because that is the time you must concentrate on getting the information down coherently. After you have done a "data dump" meaning concentrating on getting all your ideas down on paper you can return to the draft and clean up the errors and mistakes.

When you are peer editing a classmate's or a friend's paper, do not focus on surface errors until after you have properly weighed in on the content, the material, and the format.

Technology Toolbox

Peer Revision with Track Changes and Comments

The "Track Changes" and "Comment" features are enormously helpful if you ask a friend to critique your writing or your professor assigns peer revision as part of a writing assignment. Each user who makes changes or inserts comments into an electronic document can be specifically identified by your word processing program. Since the changes each person makes will be assigned a different color, using these features will allow you to easily see which edits you made yourself or which of your reviewers fixed a typo or made a suggestion.

Level 1

Name_____ **Date**_____

DIRECTIONS Each of the following sections has been written for a general audience. Read the passage, choose the audience most appropriate for the subject matter, and revise the passage to address the person or group you have chosen. Before writing, define your audience.

SAMPLE

Audience: everyone

Studies show exercise is good for the human body, and the greater the intensity, the better. Accordingly, everyone should work out for at least one hour a day, with at least half of the hour doing aerobics like running or biking. If everyone would follow this simple regime, health care costs would drop dramatically and Americans would lose the fat and gain the fitness.

Revised:

Audience: school children, ages 10–18

Each week a new study reveals that intense exercise helps students lower their weight, improve their health and self-esteem, and create long-term habits for responsible living. Many kids come home from school, have an unhealthy snack like potato chips, and sit down in front of the computer or television, but this is an easy habit to break. Instead, eat a banana or piece of fruit for energy and go for a bike ride, a run, or participate in after school sports and activities.

1. Audience: teacher

Students should come to school prepared to learn, and this means entering class with their homework done, with the books and supplies they need for class, dressed appropriately, well fed, and attentive. When half of the class has not done their homework, did not bring their books, have to borrow materials, and are disruptive by sleeping or talking, they disturb the learning process for those who want to do well.

_____

_____

2. Audience: general

Crimes against the elderly have become more frequent as the baby boomers live longer. What is happening when family members neglect or abuse their elderly parent or grandparent by withholding medications, food, or administering beatings? What does this say about our society? Elder abuse must be stopped. These people once led productive lives and raised families, so don't throw them out with the trash.

_____

_____

3. Audience: people who read the newspaper

Every day there is more violence in the Middle East. Most recently, Israel and Lebanon are bombing each other frequently, and innocent men, women, and children pay the price with their lives and health. There must be some way to achieve peace, though many presidents and world leaders have tried repeatedly.

_____

_____

4. Audience: U.S. citizens

To reduce our landfills we must be willing to go under mandatory recycling programs. People who will not conform to the recycling request would be fined heavily and repeatedly until they began using their recycle bins appropriately. Every day billions of tons of garbage go into the landfills and at least half of the waste is bottles, cans, and plastics that could be recycled. Stop being lazy and start recycling!

_____

_____

Level 1

Name_____ **Date**_____

DIRECTIONS Revise each section by rewriting with stronger word choices that clarify meaning. Get creative with your revisions to improve these passages.

SAMPLE

The Arctic Monkeys are a popular band right now. They are from England and have become popular in the U.S. It is probably due to a fan's *Myspace* site that posted some songs and lyrics.

Enjoying the wave of popularity in both the U.S. and Great Britain, the Arctic Monkeys credit some of their success in the U.S. to a fan's Myspace Web site.

1. It is okay to be an individual instead of a member of a group or clique. People are too quick to buy the latest trend or get the latest haircut instead of just being good with who they are. Being part of a clique is hard because there is a lot of pressure. When you are not in a clique, you have no one to answer to.

   _____

   _____

2. Downloading music is still controversial even if most are buying the tracks and CDs. This is probably due to the fact that some are still not getting their music the legal way. These people are saying it should be hard or impossible to do that, but isn't that blaming the technology for the crime?

   _____

   _____

3. It is becoming harder for people to live on minimum wage. Maybe Congress should try living on minimum wage and see how they like it when they can't pay their bills or eat anything but cheap stuff. The minimum wage should be higher. Congress should vote for that.

   _____

   _____

Level 1

Name_____ Date_____

DIRECTIONS Rewrite each section so that concepts and terms are clear.

SAMPLE

Identity theft has become a huge problem. The Internet makes it easier for people to commit identity theft. People willingly give credit information in emails thinking the emails are real. Others shop on non-secure sites. All of this makes identity theft more common.

Stealing someone's personal information like name and social security number to commit fraudulent acts is called identity theft, one of the fastest growing crimes in the nation. Computers enable consumers to innocently pass along important financial information like their names and social security numbers through bogus email solicitations and non-secure Web sites.

1. Recumbent bikes are making a comeback. They are bikes made for the rider's comfort. The seat is larger, handlebars are located higher, and the pedals are more forward for a comfortable ride. The style was made popular in the 1800s but a racing controversy caused them to be banned from racing. Recently they have made a comeback.

   _____

   _____

2. Inline skating is a big individual sport. It is also called rollerblading, but Rollerblade is actually a company and not the activity. Some like inline skates because they are designed to go faster with less effort than traditional skates. The first inline skate was invented in 1700 when a Dutch guy nailed wooden spools to his shoes.

   _____

   _____

3. Ice fishing is a popular sport in the winter in northern states with lakes. You have to wait until a lake freezes hard enough to hold human weight. There are several fishing pole styles to choose from because ice fishing is different from warm weather fishing. People use an auger to cut the hole in the lake. The fish like the warmest water, so shallow areas are best.

   _____

   _____

4. Target archers are bow and arrow users who shoot at targets. 3 D archery is like golf because the archer must guess the distance correctly to hit the target. Depending on the preference, the bow can be simple fiberglass or complex composite with wheels and pulleys. Tips were once made out of animal bone or rocks but today's tips are alloy and steel.

_____

_____

5. Like baseball, women's fast pitch softball is a game of great excitement. Traditional softball pitchers pitched underhand, but fast pitch pitchers pitch overhand up to 70 miles per hour. Women's softball teams are in just about every high school, college, and university. There are professional leagues too. Like baseball, people on base can steal bases.

_____

_____

Level 1

Name_____ **Date**_____

DIRECTIONS Revise each section so that its tone is appropriate for a general audience.

SAMPLE

Gosh, making a peanut butter sandwich is child's play! Get a couple of pieces of yummy bread, your ab fab peanut butter, and a knife and you're in business.

Making a peanut butter sandwich is one of the easiest dishes to prepare. Simply gather two pieces of bread, a jar of peanut butter, and a knife.

1. If there was ever a doubt about who wrote the works of Shakespeare, think no further. Scholars in the field have long known Shakespeare was the one and only playwright and poet, despite amateurs and gossip hounds who sought to cheapen the Bard's accomplishments with weak scholarship and watery claims.

_____

_____

2. Clearly, Ernest Hemingway was a man's man writer, no wimp or milquetoast like F. Scott Fitzgerald. Hemingway's characters behaved like gentlemen and lived by a code of ethics, but Fitzgerald's were silly imposters who had no values or morals. It is crazy to think that these guys were even friends when Hemingway's men were awesome and Fitzgerald's were sleazy.

_____

_____

3. People who believe that the country should maintain Daylight Savings Time have lost their minds. We are no longer an agrarian culture, so most kids don't head off into the fields after 7th period. Since half of America seems to suffer from depression during the winter, here's a novel idea: keep the time that gives us the longest amount of daylight! The government needs to ignore the whiners, make the decision to give us the best time schedule and call it a day.

_____

_____

Level 2

Name_____ **Date**_____

DIRECTIONS Revise each of the following examples to appeal to a different audience, using a different tone, and writing for a different purpose. Specify the audience, tone, and purpose you have in mind.

SAMPLE

Tooth care in this country lags behind other major forms of health care. In fact, the number of children and adults walking around today with rotten teeth and cavities that need filling is atrocious and shameful. Insurance should cover this serious problem.

Dental hygiene takes a back seat to other forms of health care in this country, and health care conglomerates at the urging of businesses and employers must reverse this alarming trend. If dental health were a priority with our health care systems and employers, the number of children and adults with untreated tooth decay would quickly drop, giving the nation's workers a healthier advantage.

1. There's a new sheriff in town and its called wikindex, an online bibliographic index that lets users store their research quotes, sources, and cool stuff for free. Today's savvy students and faculty are on the down low with technology that saves them from the tedious pen and paper. Go see the new sheriff at http://wikindx.sourceforge.net/

   _____

   _____

2. Internet shopping has become a breeze, and many buyers are rejecting the hustle and bustle of the malls for the comfort of shopping through the computer. Holidays or birthdays? A few clicks of the mouse and some credit card information and your special gift arrives at a loved one's door in a few days. You can even have a "personalized" gift card attached and have your special purchase gift wrapped.

   _____

   _____

3. The computer has revolutionized communication as we know it today, and the results are incredibly controversial. On the one hand, people write each other more than ever, using email, online chats, cyber clubs or organizations, and text messaging. On the other hand, when people prefer to message each other instead of walking down the hall for a face to face conversation, there is a problem. This problem is the breakdown of normal conversations.

_____

_____

4. Today's cyber criminal is a faceless coward who preys on faceless people in creepy ways. Hackers think it is funny to get into people's computers to steal their passwords and financial information. Tons of hackers write programs that get sent out over email. These worms can wipe out a hard drive in the snap of a finger. Depending on the person, one stupid "joke" can ruin a person's life.

_____

_____

5. New cars of a certain level of sophistication come with the technology to interface with cellular phones, MP3 players, DVD players and other exterior technical devices to aid in the passenger's pleasures. Prior to the trip to the grocery store or across the country, drivers and passengers can personalize the voyage with customized music selections, a ready phone list of contacts, and specific movies to coincide with the journey. Car travel takes on a whole new level.

_____

_____

Writing with Technology

The Thomson Handbook, **Chapters 24, 25**

Word processing programs like *Microsoft Word, AppleWorks,* and *WordPerfect* enable authors of all levels to infuse their works with simple to complex applications to exemplify, enhance, and elaborate points in their texts and papers. Whereas the term paper of yesterday was always 12 point Times New Roman, today's writers engage technology to blur the boundaries between traditional print discourse and visual design.

When reading this chapter and Chapters 24 and 25 in *The Thomson Handbook,* keep in mind that your single most important responsibility is to keep your audience's needs in front of your design choices and options.

As you review the material in this chapter, which spans the rudimentary to the complex in desktop publishing, always remember the main rule of thumb when engaging technology: make it practical and useful for your audience. In other words, never employ technology just because you can. For example, choose fonts that are easy to read and images that complement the text.

Maximizing Papers with Fonts, Lists, and Emphases

Fonts

Typography, the use of **fonts** (Verdana, Bradley Hand ITC, Comic Sans MS, Arial, and so forth), *italics,* underlines, CAPITAL LETTERS, **boldface,** or *A COMBINATION* clearly sets some text apart from the rest of the mostly uniform presentations that we associate with traditional college writing. **If you experiment with fonts and typographical elements in your paper, remain consistent and do not overwhelm your reader.**

Never mix font styles within one paper, desktop design, or Web page. A paper that is too busy becomes distracting and difficult to read.

Just like you must choose a specific audience, write with a purpose, and use a deliberate tone or attitude, when considering fonts different from the standard 12 point Times New Roman, you must reconcile how this choice will affect your work. For example, if you select a playful font for a formal paper like Curz MT because you like how it looks, it is likely that your professor and your peers may disagree with your aesthetics. Also, you should not use the larger fonts for assignments that have required page lengths. For example Verdana in 12 point, Bookman Old Style in 12 point, and Century Gothic in 12 point are much larger than Times New Roman in 12 point.

Always check with your professor before you experiment with fonts to make sure your intentions match the assignment and purpose.

However, for a journal assignment with a word count specification, experiment with matching your mood, tone, and attitude with a font to further enhance both the writing experience for yourself and the reading experience for your audience. Always make sure the font is readable for your intended audience.

Lauren Friedman,
Journal Response
October 31, 2006

> You asked us to reflect on today's holiday, Halloween, and I want to take you back, way back to a time of innocence when I was a child. The date: October 31, 1990. I was dressed as a princess and my brother, Joel, was a pirate, or at least that is what we thought. At the time our parents did not have much money, so our costumes were homemade from the rag bag and whatever else my mom could find, but we thought we were the real deal...

In this example Lauren could use the "Chiller" font to imitate and reflect the Halloween mood and festivities she describes in her journal assignment.

Fonts are categorized as either *serif* or *sans serif*. The serif fonts have small decorative elements like points or extra ends and are traditional to print discourse; they include Times New Roman, Harrington, Courier, Bookman Old Style, and Palatino.

Sans serif means without the small decorative elements; these fonts are more likely seen in non-traditional mediums like Web pages and brochures. Common san serif fonts include Verdana, Arial, and Century Gothic.

Lists

Lists help readers to visually understand text they may otherwise have overlooked. These brief catalogs help the audience categorize a number of items more quickly than if they were in traditional sentence form. When using either the numbered or bulleted format, keep the information short and remain consistent in punctuation, parallelism, and sentence style.

Information in a traditional sentence:

The lacrosse team must raise $2000 this year because they need new uniforms, they must hire a manager and an assistant, and they plan to hold a summer camp for local area players next summer.

Inconsistent list:
The lacrosse team must raise $2000 this year to pay for:

- new uniforms

- a manager and an assistant

- Next summer they want to host a summer camp for local area players.

(*The last sentence is non-parallel with the other two and has a period at the end.*)

Consistent list:
The lacrosse team must raise $2000 this to pay for:

- new uniforms

- a manager and an assistant

- a summer camp

Numbered lists are useful in describing a set or sequence of instructions or steps.

The lacrosse team can raise the money needed by completing the following:

1. Secure corporate sponsors from community businesses
2. Hold weekly bake sales in student union
3. Hire themselves out for Rent-a-Student promotion
4. Conduct occasional car washes

The process of electing a Student Government President is as follows:

1. An individual must declare interest
2. Student Senate must determine eligibility
3. Eligible entrants must be granted a 15-day campaign opportunity
4. All candidates must participate in a debate
5. The winner is determined by a majority of votes in a general election

Emphases

Emphases are <u>underscores,</u> *italics,* and **bolding** that make words pop out from the remainder of the text. Authors use these techniques sparingly, and typically apply them to key terms or phrases, ironic or coincidental instances, or as emphasis in dialogue. For example:

> In the play we are never sure if the father figure is actually dead because we only have the word of a *psychotic ghost. (The author wants the reader to understand the element of unreliability that exists with a character that is a psychotic ghost.)*
>
> Within the past few decades, vast quantities of coral have been lost due to a reaction called **bleaching**. *(The reader assumes the sentences to follow will explain in detail the process.)*
>
> The <u>procedure</u> for the experiment began with collecting twenty hand prints. *(The author marks a shift from explanation to procedure.)*
>
> When asked why she ran for President of the Animal Welfare Coalition, Cait explained, "People say we must do something, so I am here to *make things happen.*" *(The italics mark the speaker's emphasis on certain words in the sentence.)*

Headings

A **heading** is a word, term, or brief phrase set apart from the text by appearing on its own line. Authors often bold or underscore headings for additional emphasis.

For some disciplines headings provide an orderly method of organizing a paper and separate information to help your readers follow a shift from one point to another. Authors use headings to:

- Provide coherence and balance in a paper
- Identify and spotlight key terms
- Signal a shift in topic

Here are the headings Danielle Brigida used in her paper, "The Relation between Finger Span and Height" for Biology 109:

- Abstract
- Introduction
- Methods

- Results
- Conclusion

Electrifying Your Text with Visuals

When you integrate today's technology with all the traditional print skills you have learned in this workbook and *The Thomson Handbook,* you create *hybrid* texts, a combination of visual imagery and print to more clearly explain your message, your purpose, and your claims to your audience. Images—drawings, photographs, paintings, sculpture, and the like—have long been part of written discourse in most mediums except scholarly discourse until recently because authors and their audiences understand the power of visual imagery *when combined with the printed word.*

Like the language you choose, the images you embed in your papers have their own tone, attitude, and meaning; therefore you must carefully select visuals that enhance and extend your work without overpowering or confusing readers. As you will see in Chapter 21's "Rhetoric on the Web," misplaced images or images that fail to correspond to text confuse audiences.

 In Fig. 1 the text accompanying the image of the Writing Spider, *Argiope auranti,* fails to explain why the visual is present in the paper. This is an example of a gratuitous use of technology because the text does not explain why the image has been embedded in the paper when the author could have just as easily given a Web address for readers to consult.

Fig. 1 reprinted by permission of Mary Wright

At left, the Writing Spider in her web.

In Fig. 2 the copy with the image of the Writing Spider, *Argiope auranti,* complements the text by providing an appropriate explanation of a written description. The text refers to the positioning of the spider's legs as well as the visible zigzag "thread" in the web.

 As noted in Fig. 1, when in her web, the Writing Spider prefers to remain in the very center as opposed to off to the side like other spider species. As if she understands this strategy might cost her in the amount of prey she catches, she typically puts her legs together to appear to have less and therefore looks smaller than she actually is.

Additionally, she creates a *stabilimentum,* the white zigzag stripe **seen in the picture left**. *Argiope auranti* remains in the stabilimentum until her web begins to vibrate with her catch. Scientists are still unclear regarding the stabilimentum's function other than to perhaps stabilize the web's center.

Fig. 2 reprinted by permission of Mary Wright

Without the image, readers who wanted a visual representation would have to consult a textbook or the Internet, but here the image and the description provide a full service.

As 24d in *The Thomson Handbook* explains, it is acceptable to use screenshots of Web pages, films, and television shows to demonstrate or analyze a point, and you do not need permission from the owner, but you still must record the information for your Works Cited page.

To avoid copyright issues, try to choose images that are freeware, which you can find on the Web by doing a search for "free images." Some Web sites like Morguefile (a newspaper term referring to old papers), available at http://www.morguefile.com, have freeware photography.

Regardless of whether your images or pages are part of the public domain, always record the url or owner's information, and for copyright purposes, make sure you contact the image or Web page author for permission.

Technology Toolbox

Embedding Screenshots

There may be times when you are working in an online environment and you want to imbed a replica of the screen into your paper to help your audience visualize your point. This process is quite easy and involves just a few simple steps:

For a PC

1. Activate your cursor in the screen you want to capture.
2. Press the "Print Screen Sys Rq" button next to the "Scroll Lock" button to copy
3. Open a new page in your word processor and either CTR V or right click to Paste the image into your document

For a Mac

1. Activate your cursor in the screen you want to capture
2. Press Apple (Command) Key + Shift + 3 to copy the entire page or
3. Press Apple (Command) Key + Shift + 4 to turn your mouse into a pointer. Drag over the portion of the screen and let go when you have gathered all you need.
4. Press Apple (Command) Key + Spacebar and the image will be transported to your desktop and labeled "Picture 1" or so on.
5. Open the image in Preview
6. Press Apple (Command) Key + V to paste the image into your document

For more information on fair use and copyrights, refer to Chapter 24 in *The Thomson Handbook*.

Inserting Pictures, Graphs, and Other Visual Enhancements

In the case of the Writing Spider, the author inserted her own photograph. Because digital cameras are less expensive to use and most computers come with photo enhancement software, personal jpgs or jpegs (joint photographic experts group), the standard format by which photos are created and saved, are easy to create and manipulate.

However, photographs are not the only images that are pertinent to a visually enhanced paper. Authors create graphs, charts, diagrams, and tables to repackage complex or difficult information, statistics, or collected experiment results in a visually understandable manner.

Many stock images are available through your computer's "Clip Art" feature found in "Insert," but most people custom design their graphics using tables and other features in their word processing program.

Here is a chart illustrating financial earnings for the Animal Welfare Coalition

First Quarter	Second Quarter	Third Quarter	Fourth Quarter	Totals
$36.85	$91.73	$137.50	$21.00	$287.08
Bake Sale	T-Shirt Sales	Donation Campaign	Bake Sale	Fundraisers

From this chart Cait and the other group members can see at a glance which events were most profitable and in which quarters the group was most active. They can use this information to revise their strategies as well as concentrate greater energies.

Here is the same information in text form:

> In the first quarter of the year, we made $36.85 at a bake sale. In the second quarter, we sold t-shirts and collected $91.73. Third quarter donations from local businesses totaled $137.50, and a fourth quarter bake sale netted us $21.00. Total money we raised for the year: $287.08.

Though just as informative and maybe more detailed, the reader must work harder to see trends, slumps, and patterns in the text version.

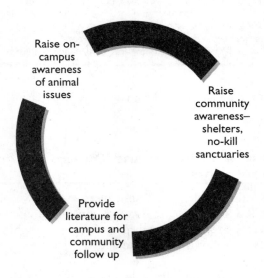

This diagram demonstrates the Animal Welfare Coalition's ongoing Awareness Campaign, which is the group's central goal.

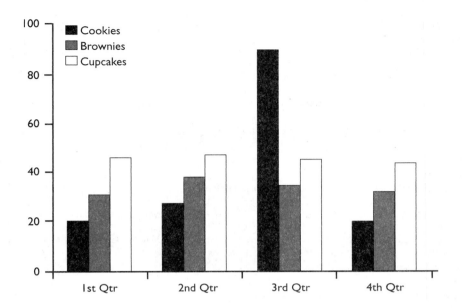

In this chart the group breaks down which items sell better at their bake sales, and can see that although cookie sales spiked in the third quarter, cupcakes are the consistent best seller.

Creating Diagrams, Charts, and Graphs

Your word processor contains ready-made diagram and chart templates, which are typically called "Objects." If you are unfamiliar with this medium, use the Help feature or perform a Web search using a keyword search like: "how to make a graph in Word" to get countless tips and advice from other users.

Desktop Publishing

In journalism, communications, technical writing, business writing, and art classes you will undoubtedly be encouraged or required to alter the traditional printed paper format you are used to by working in the desktop publishing format, which employs a combination of graphics and text in newspaper, magazine, brochure, or newsletter style. Skills you learn and perfect will help you after you graduate as many college graduates find themselves working on desktop published documents for their employers. This communication medium has grown in exciting ways.

For training purposes, *Microsoft Word* contains a variety of simple templates or fill-in-the-blank patterns. Macintosh users have *Apple Pages,* and *QuarkXPress* and *Macromedia PageMaker* work on both operating systems. Regardless of the software program employed, writers must apply the same principles to desktop writing as they do to traditional print writing: focus on the intended audience and be clear about the purpose. Chapter 25 in *The Thomson Handbook* demonstrates some of the creative choices an author may engage in this field.

Making a Brochure

To make a brochure, which you will need to do to complete the Level Two exercise at the end of this chapter, in *Word* go to "File," choose "Page Setup," and then the "Margins" tab. Midway down the box you will see "Multiple Pages," which has a dropdown menu bar. Choose "Book fold" from the list.

To customize your brochure with color, go to "Format" and then "Background," where a color palette lets you pick the tint most appropriate to the assignment.

Since no brochure would be complete without pictures or images, go to "Insert," then "Picture," to liven up your project with images to complement the text.

Level 1

Name_____ Date_____

DIRECTIONS Each of the following examples has been written in a different font. Analyze and evaluate whether the font choice is appropriate for the message and explain why or why not by interpreting the font's relationship to the tone, audience, and purpose of the message.

SAMPLE

In our initial meeting we observed the gorilla subjects to be nervous and unsure of their surroundings. When zookeepers entered the room the subjects became markedly agitated and were unable to calm down.

It is the recommendation of this committee that the gorillas be moved from this particular zoo immediately to protect their health and place the zoo on a watch list for further infractions.

The font seems too informal and relaxed for such a serious memo regarding the apparent mistreatment of animals and the serious recommendations the author suggested.

1. *Mr. and Mrs. Eugene W. Wright cordially invite you to high tea to be served on March 5, 2006 at 4:00 p.m. The occasion marks their daughter's birthday. Dress is semi-formal and guests should R.S.V.P. no later than February 3, 2006.*

   _____

   _____

2. In order to explore some of the perceptions and misconceptions about work, I have conducted an interview of my grandmother, a full time homemaker, and my grandfather, a recently retired orthopedic surgeon of 40 years.

   _____

   _____

3. **IN RESPONSE TO THE HOMEWORK ASSIGNMENT I WISH TO SAY I THOUGHT THE WILLA CATHER NOVEL, <u>MY ANTONIA</u> WAS LOVELY. UNREQUITED LOVE, HOW SOLID FRIENDSHIP CAN TURN INTO SOMETHING MORE, RESPONSIBILITIES TO OTHERS, ALL OF THESE ARE THEMES I STRONGLY BELIEVE IN.**

   _____

   _____

Level 1

Name_____ **Date**_____

DIRECTIONS Read through the traditional texts and use the space provided to create either a bulleted or numbered list. Revise the text to create appropriate parallel structure and tone.

SAMPLE

On her list of graduation presents she wanted, Cindy listed a trip to Key West, a manicure and pedicure, some new clothes, and she said she wanted a convertible sports car.

Cindy's list of graduation presents included:

- A trip to Key West
- A manicure and pedicure
- New clothes
- A convertible sports car

1. In order to pass Business Writing Ann needs to write a grant proposal for a local business, take 3 make-up quizzes, and there is a final paper. She is also missing 2 homework assignments.

_____

_____

2. Cheryl frequently takes her vacations on the Massachusetts cape because she is a beach lover. She goes to the Mayflower, the Marconi, and Skaket. The water is warmer at Marconi, but parking is better at Skaket.

_____

_____

3. Daryl is so proud of Caroline because she has practiced hard at ballet and was accepted to a very elite ballet school in San Francisco. Caroline also dances lead in *The Nutcracker* every year.

_____

_____

4. In curling a game is called a match. Two opposing teams play each other until one scores more than the other. They play on an ice rink of official dimensions, and their equipment includes 16 round curling stones, 2 for each of the 4 players on the 2 teams. To win the object is to slide the stones in the center of a target.

_____

_____

5. When planning her big dinner party Tracey discovered there were quite a few details to iron out before the guests arrived. She needed ice for the drinks and the shrimp, appetizers to keep guests satisfied until the meal arrived, flowers for the centerpiece, and she still needed to set the table.

_____

_____

6. In her second semester freshman year, Jeanne took English, Earth Science, Intro to Business, Statistics, and Pottery. From those classes she realized she was going to major in business and minor in English because she could write well, loved the business class, did very well in Statistics, and was less interested in pottery and science.

_____

_____

7. When she can Kate enjoys going to the university's gym for a workout. She begins her workout with a 2 mile run on the treadmill or outside when the weather is nice. Then she spends about 30 minutes on free weights for upper body strength, does 100 sit ups, and finishes her routine on the elliptical trainer.

_____

_____

Level 1

Name_____ Date_____

DIRECTIONS For this exercise you must use your computer's word processor and have access to a printer. Following are several traditional text scenarios. Rewrite them on your word processor and create headings where you think they are appropriate and add any emphases when necessary.

1. Kristin has written a draft that she needs to revise into a paper with headings. She interviewed her grandparents, Dorothy and Earl, about how they define *work*. She began by introducing them to her audience as a homemaker and a retired orthopedic surgeon, respectively, discussed their history as productive members of society, as parents, as grandparents, and as workers. Then Kristin focused on the role of the homemaker, asking her grandmother why she chose to stay at home instead of work and raise a family. Through Dorothy's answers, Kristin decided that the homemaker duties were equally important as occupations outside of the home, and finished her paper discussing how a single income can strain the family if the adults have not agreed ahead of time on the situation.

2. Danielle wrote a draft in which she read and analyzed a textbook on "global capitalism and its negative effects." In her draft she began with a quotation from the text that she believed adequately defined global capitalism as people and countries competing for the lowest wage while causing greater environmental harm. She discussed main ideas the authors considered in the book such as the downside of globalization (poor working conditions, cutbacks in services, accelerated destruction of the environment) and positive elements of global capitalism (expanded the wealth of a few hundred corporations). She then observed how her Biology class covered some of these issues, like poverty in underdeveloped countries, population problems, and destruction of forests and pollution. She ended her draft by giving solutions to the problem like limit growth in underdeveloped countries, concentrate on humane ways to build the global economy, use fewer resources, responsibly develop poorer countries, and pay decent wages.

Level 1

Name_____ **Date**_____

DIRECTIONS For this exercise you must use your computer's word processor and have access to a printer to submit your work. Read the following scenarios and revise them from text format to visual format. You may use graphs, pie charts, images, or anything you believe will enhance the information in the text, but you may not reuse the same option more than once (only one graph, one pie chart, one diagram, etc).

1. Katie finds herself unable to manage her time between soccer games and practice, school responsibilities, relaxation time, and family, so she needs to analyze how she spends her time. She determines that she practices for soccer 15 hours a week, attends school 20 hours a week, does homework 5 hours a week, spends time with her family 5 hours a week, and goes out with friends 7 hours a week.

2. Caroline, Katie's sister, does not think she has a time management problem, but she decided to chart her time too. Caroline plays soccer and runs for the cross country team. She practices soccer 10 hours a week, practices cross country 8 hours a week, attends school 23 hours a week, works on homework 9 hours a week, spends time with her family 3 hours a week, and hangs out with friends 8 hours a week.

3. Spencer and Drew share their toys when their parents remind them, but as little boys they are still learning responsibility. Their parents need a visual device so the boys will have equal time with their toys, but first they observed the children playing with the following items in these times for the week:

Bow and arrow	Drew: 90 minutes.	Spencer: 45 minutes
Scooter	Drew: 75 minutes.	Spencer: 100 minutes
Bike	Drew: 100 minutes	Spencer: 40 minutes
Light saber	Drew: 60 minutes	Spencer: 60 minutes

Level 2

Name_____ **Date**_____

DIRECTIONS Use the information you learned in this chapter to create a brochure about yourself. You will find instructions for formatting a brochure in the last Technology Toolbox. Be creative! For example, your brochure might cover multiple aspects of you, such as your major, classes you are taking, clubs and activities you are in, as well as your hobbies, goals, and experiences. Remember, you cannot use any images from the Internet that are copyright protected.

Visual and Oral Presentations

The Thomson Handbook, Chapter 26

There will be many occasions where you will be asked to give an oral presentation or turn a written paper into either a speech or oral presentation with visual enhancements. Think of such an assignment as another revision of a draft in which you adjust your audience, purpose, and style while employing a different set of tools and medium.

Following are comparisons between the written and spoken/visual options that should help you see the difference in the communication patterns.

The Author's Options	**The Speaker's Options**
Present introductory material and thesis to answer reader expectations	Present introductory material and thesis to answer listener expectations
Sentences are not governed by any length.	Sentences should be short
	Repetition to reinforce memorability
Free to employ a variety of rhetorical devices	Less choice in complicated rhetorical devices
Text is available for reader review	Audience must remember & follow along
Conclude with reminding audience of points presented in paper	Conclude with reminding audience of points presented in paper
Must guess at audience	Can see audience and adjust message
Ample time to present paper and purpose	Limited time to present paper and purpose
No performance anxiety!	Probable performance anxiety!

The Reader's Options	**The Listener's Options**
Freedom to read and reread	One opportunity to receive message
No time limit in reading	Must follow speaker's time constraints
No option for immediate feedback	May debate and converse with speaker

The chart on page 590 in *The Thomson Handbook* can help you determine your role as the speaker/author and your audience's new role as a listener and not just a reader.

The Importance of Memory

In ancient Greece, people routinely memorized book-length treatises and recited them perfectly. The philosopher Quintilian claimed, "Our whole education depends upon memory." The Greeks saw memory as a teachable gift, and Plato predicted that writing would not only replace oral communication but also diminish our need for memory. He was right because even though we still memorize for tests, for oral presentations, and for our own personal enjoyment (sports statistics, dialog from our favorite movies, things people say to us), very few people can actually recite Homer's *The Odyssey* today. Why should we, when we have the printed text?

What we learn from Plato helps us plan our oral and visual presentations because the reader has the opportunity to review what she or he has previously read *whereas the listener must rely on memory*. This means the speaker must clearly announce purpose and intentions, and sustain the audience through carefully staged verbal cues.

Speaking Strategies

When preparing an oral presentation with or without visual devices, you must consider your audience's capacity to remember your speech, which means you must make your speech memorable by using *mnemonics* or memory-enhancing strategies.

Repetition of a word or idea keeps concepts fresh in listeners' minds. Martin Luther King Jr.'s "I Have a Dream" speech riveted his audience that hot August day at the Lincoln Memorial in 1963. Toward the end of his speech eight consecutive paragraphs begin with "I have a dream," and these paragraphs contain the phrase, "Let freedom ring." The entire speech is a rhetorical masterpiece, but it shall be known in U.S. history for those two phrases which were King's memory-enhancing strategy.

Brevity in sentence structure is a must for both the speaker and the listener to keep track of important points. When the speaker uses complex sentences, listeners forget the beginning and often lose the central point. Consider Mike Hilleary's first sentence in his paper:

> Perception in the sense of understanding one's own ever-evolving cultural history and development has always seemed to hold with it some undeniable implication of being somewhat inclusive, something that theoretically can be easily accessed and understood without any restrictive hindrances.

In speech form, the sentence might sound like:

> We should not restrict ourselves to accessing and understanding our constantly evolving cultural histories.

Hit three to four key points. Explain very early how many points you plan to present so your listeners will be attentive to hearing each one. Your speech should whet your audience's appetites for more information, which they can get from you after you finish, typically in question-and-answer periods that follow oral presentations. Unlike a paper where you have the luxury of elaboration, pick the most pertinent issues your audience needs to hear in order to follow you. Like many thrilling orators throughout history, Dr. Martin Luther King, Jr. had ample time to orate in "I Have a Dream" about the reasons why he needed to be standing in front of the crowd at that particular moment, and he explains in the first few paragraphs how, despite strides made in history such as the Emancipation Proclamation, "But one hundred years later, the Negro is still not free." You, however, will probably not stand before an attentive crowd fixated on such a tremendous moment in politics and cultural history, at least not in your college-level presentations, but your choice in mnemonics is still important.

If your topic is the reasons why your fellow classmates should vote for you for freshman class president, you need to literally hand them the reasons why they should listen to you and give you their votes.

- Steve Konikoff is always ready to listen to your concerns.
- Steve Konikoff will actively participate in student government affairs.
- Steve Konikoff will host more social events for freshmen.
- Steve Konikoff has political experience.

Bullets and Lists

To create bulleted and/or numbered lists simply choose one or the other from the "Toolbar" at the top of your screen or select from the "Format" drop-down menu.

After entering the information for the first item, hit "Enter" and another bullet will automatically appear. When you are finished, double "Enter" to disengage the automatic list feature.

Creating Visual Rhetoric

When creating a visual aid you must keep one central idea in mind at all times: is this actually useful to my audience? If your pretty *PowerPoint* presentation, slide show, or poster simply parrots what you say, you have wasted your time and materials.

All visual content must **enhance, elaborate,** and lend **detail** to the spoken word, never simply repeat.

Print Rhetoric	**Visual Rhetoric**
Typical Beginning, Middle, End	Typical Beginning, Middle, End
Text is utmost important	Text is utmost important
All visual references must be described	Visual images complement text
Text is black on white paper	Text and background can be any color
Less option for creativity if appropriate	Tremendous options for creativity if appropriate

Visual rhetoric **complements** the oral presentation, so think of your visual aid as something that briefly echoes your spoken performance.

You Say	**Your Visual Aid Says**
Steve Konikoff is always ready to listen to your concerns.	Your voice will be heard
Steve Konikoff will actively participate in student government affairs.	Your representative works for you
Steve Konikoff will host more social events for freshmen	Your social calendar is filling fast
Steve Konikoff has political experience	Your representative is experienced

Publishing software includes *PowerPoint* for Windows and Mac users and *iWork* for Mac users. Both enable the user to create interactive content; embed visual and audio images and files; and create colorful presentations with special effects. If your personal computer does not have either program and you are interested in them, check with your campus I.T. Services department for available options. See page 592 in *The Thomson Handbook* for an example of a *PowerPoint* presentation.

Slideshow software like *PowerPoint*, *Apple Keynote*, and *Adobe Acrobat Professional* enable users to provide sharp visual aids and distill their message into talking points, those bulleted snippets the audience can read while the speaker elaborates in greater detail. While each program provides a variety of colorful templates, you can create your own quite easily to enhance your presentation's memorability. However, **never let technology upstage the speaker.** When your audience becomes more enamored with your presentation than your speech, you have lost them!

Overhead Transparencies are less flashy versions of slides that the speaker manually places on a projector. Instead of being saved in a file, the speaker has physical transparency pages, and thus greater control should technology fail. A great feature about this option is that during the presentation, the speaker can write on the transparency, editing or revising the information to include, for example, audience feedback.

Posters provide a more permanent and stable visual presentation of your points. Many conferences have poster sessions where audience members can file throughout rooms of posters to read the content at their own pace. Posters can be as elaborate as a three-part foldout or as simple as one page.

Smart Cart and Digital Classroom situations enable the speaker to utilize any form of digital media for the presentation, from a Web site to a slide show, or something done with presentation software. The caveat: your disk or jump drive must be compatible with the existing hardware and software.

Chalk and White Board options enable the speaker to write talking points, research references, or other important text in advance, as well as to write during the presentation and follow-up discussion. This is the most temporary of all choices because the material must be copied in order to leave the room.

A good orator mixes up the choices, trying one strategy with each option until finding the most comfortable and appropriate fit. Always have a backup plan in case technology fails, because it will. Ask Danielle Brigida, who was evaluating a Web site for her class when the power failed!

Level 1

Name_____ **Date**_____

DIRECTIONS Help Kristin revise each written chunk into speech bullets or talking points.

SAMPLE

When asked what sexual harassment is, most people conjure up the image of a male boss making lewd comments toward a female employee or requesting sexual favors. However, most do not have an image involving two men horsing around at a worksite. The line that designates which of these scenarios constitutes harassment is a blurry one at best because many are unsure of the defining characteristics of the behavior. However, with an increasing number of men claiming that they have been abused by other men, it's time to take a closer look at the issue.

- Most define sexual harassment as a male boss making lewd comments to female employees
- Most do not see harassment between two male employees
- Definitions of sexual harassment are blurry
- Rising cases of male to male harassment warrant looking closely at the issue

1. There are some who do not believe that the "male on male" variety is truly a form of sexual harassment. For example, at construction sites, a fair amount of horseplay takes place. Employees claim that this behavior occurs every day. This type of behavior can help to alleviate stress on the job, lifting the spirits of the employees. Productivity increases when the staff is relaxed and happy; therefore, this type of play is acceptable and even useful.

_____

_____

2. However, not everyone agrees that workplace antics are appropriate. Some employees are uncomfortable by the actions of their coworkers. This is not to say that they have not engaged in their share of roughhousing after working in many shipyards and construction sites. They claim they would "horseplay a bit at lunchtime"; however their definition of the activity involved adolescent pranks played on other employees such as putting black tape over someone's visor, hiding lunches, banging loudly on the john, and so forth.

_____

_____

3. When "horseplay" begins to affect someone's job performance, it has become something more than just play. If an action makes someone uncomfortable, it is sexual harassment. The number of male on male sexual harassment cases continues to climb, and the confusion as to what to do in each situation mounts. A suggested solution would be to have individual companies decide where to draw the line between sexual harassment and horseplay. Steps such as these will greatly help to make clear what is considered acceptable behavior in the workplace.

_____

_____

Level 1

Name_____ Date_____

DIRECTIONS Write four sentences (talking points) that will be memorable to your audience for each of the following topics.

SAMPLE

>   Vote in the next school election
>   You can be part of a change to be proud of
>   You can change the way our school is governed
>   You can change how others perceive politics
>   Vote in the next school election to become part of a positive change

1. The importance of dental hygiene

   _____

   _____

   _____

   _____

2. Tips for buying a used car

   _____

   _____

   _____

   _____

3. The best vacation place for little money

   _____

   _____

   _____

   _____

4. The attributes of a good student

_____

_____

_____

_____

5. How to be a conscientious tourist

_____

_____

_____

_____

Level 1

Name_____ Date_____

DIRECTIONS Revise the following talking points so they become visual aids for a speech presentation, such as a slide show, transparency showing, or *PowerPoint* or *iWork* presentation. Feel free to rearrange for clarity.

SAMPLE

Bicycle safety has been ignored in the community long enough
Auto collisions with bike riders resulted in 17 deaths, 11 injuries in 2006
The public must be educated for future safety
We need more bike lanes on main thoroughfares

Bicyclers in crisis
17 deaths, 11 injuries in 2006
Public education a must
Marked bike lanes for major streets

1. Horseback riding is a sport and a leisure activity
   Depending on the purpose, some horses are trained to race
   Horse farms in Kentucky occupy much of the countryside
   Many non-professional events are available for competition

   _____

   _____

   _____

   _____

2. Is air travel safer in 2006 than it was in 2001?
   Increases in airport security stop threats
   More training for baggage handlers make luggage safer
   Bomb sniffing dogs at most major airports

   _____

   _____

   _____

   _____

3. Auto racing is a popular sport in sections of the U.S.
   Several styles of racing appeal to fan factions
   Major corporate sponsors help popularize the sport
   Fan base is strong and dedicated

   _____

   _____

   _____

   _____

4. Hot air balloons are a beautiful way to experience flying
   Balloons are fueled by propane tanks that heat air
   Ground crew and pilot coordinate liftoff
   Flying and landing must be in clear spaces
   Enjoy flying 30,000 feet high

   _____

   _____

   _____

   _____

5. Amusement park fans love the bumper cars
   Easy to maneuver for people of all ages
   Teaches driving skills to kids
   Lets patrons enjoy the "crash"

   _____

   _____

   _____

   _____

Level 1

Name _____ Date _____

DIRECTIONS Read each of the following rhetorical scenarios; conduct brief research; and determine the audience, purpose, and medium (which visual presentation). Sketch out three talking points and explain which visual aid you would employ to complement your oral discussion. Describe the visual presentation.

SAMPLE

How to Properly Trim a Crepe Myrtle Tree
Audience: Homeowners with crepe myrtle trees
Purpose: Dispel myths and demonstrate proper techniques
Medium: Slideshow

Talking Points:
Previous advice called for butchering tree and weakening following season's growth
Selective pruning beginning after the tree has bloomed, preferably winter or early spring
Choose 4–7 strongest limbs and prune out the rest

Slideshow Medium:
Slides of badly pruned trees and explain problems
Slides of untouched tree in late winter before cutting
Slides identifying strongest branches and actual pruning

1. The benefits of recycling
   Audience:
   Purpose:
   Medium

   Talking Points:

   Medium:

2. How to Stay Properly Hydrated
   Audience:
   Purpose:
   Medium

   Talking Points:

   Medium:

3. How to Fix a Flat
   Audience:
   Purpose:
   Medium

   Talking Points:

   Medium:

Level 2

Name_____ **Date**_____

DIRECTIONS Chapter 3 of *The Thomson Handbook* contains student author Angela Garrison's paper entitled, "From Over There to Over Here: War Blogs Get Up Close, Personal, and Profitable" (43–46). Read Angela's paper, determine what the most important points are, and make a slideshow to turn the print version into a visual presentation. In the space below, write your outline and explain each slide. Remember, an effective visual presentation gives bulleted information for the speaker to explain orally. Ask your instructor about the best way to submit your slideshow.

SAMPLE

> Intro slide:
> What is a blog?
> How do people use blogs?
> Why blogs are popular with U.S. soldiers

Rhetoric on the Web
The Thomson Handbook, Chapters 27–32

Originally the Internet was created as a system of networks that enabled people all over the world to instantly send and receive documents written on a computer using a word processing program. This appealed to the scientific community, whose members wanted to quickly transport documents to their colleagues in other labs, other cities, and other countries. The fax or facsimile machine proved to be too slow, and emailing large or bulky documents did not work, so Tim Berners-Lee, an enterprising scientist, created Hypertext Markup Language (html), a language that browsers use to display and link Web pages.

You should note then that the Internet was originally created for *traditional text documents.* Now writers create **digital discourse,** writing meant to be read only on the Web or through an email client, which you will soon see is quite different from **print discourse,** traditional writing meant to be read in hard copy.

After the invention of html, people outside of the scientific community began taking interest in this new medium; from that point on, the Web has been as much a visual enterprise as a network of shared documents. Some of the shared documents covered in this chapter and Chapters 27–32 in *The Thomson Handbook* include **email, blogs and wikis, electronic research,** and **Web pages.**

Using Email Effectively

Some critics believe email has driven the final nail in the coffin of letter writing; others disagree, seeing email as a tool that has increased letter writing among people who otherwise would not put pen to paper. Regardless of the debate, electronic mail or email is one

Technology Toolbox

Email Etiquette
Do not mix business with pleasure. As a student, you will probably be required to communicate frequently with your professors regarding school matters. If you have not done so already, be sure to open a school email account and consider this your "business" or "professional" correspondence account.

Maintain a separate account with the provider of your choice, like *Google, Yahoo, Hotmail,* etc. to correspond with others. This way, if you have a funny email address like hot_sexy_princess1 or bad_boy_jason you will not reveal private items about yourself to professors, school administrators, and others receiving your correspondence.

Get in the habit of checking both accounts frequently so you do not miss important announcements like a change in an assignment or the meeting place of your classes.

of the most popular forms of communication used in the world today, from keeping daughter Katie who lives in Las Vegas connected with parents Mark and Pat who live in Texas, to making sure heads of nations and countries are connected with constituents.

Audience, Tone, and Purpose in Email

As 27a in *The Thomson Handbook* demonstrates, typing an email requires the same authorial considerations as typing a paper. You must **define and write to a specific audience,** and in many cases email makes that task easier because you literally address your reader in the *To:* line and most often begin your email specifically naming that person:

> Dear Dr. Rowley,
>
> or
>
> Hi Mom,

Once you have chosen your audience, use addressing conventions appropriate to the relationship you have with the person or people. Even your favorite professor, with whom you spend time chatting outside of class, should not receive an email using slang like:

> Yo, Dr. Rowley!

Just as you would never consider using formal conventions with your parents:

> Dear Mr. and Mrs. Puzz,

After selecting an audience, you then **choose the appropriate tone and attitude** to convey your message:

> Dear Dr. Rowley,
>
> Thank you again for loaning me those articles for my research paper. I appreciate your interest in my work and your willingness to help.
>
> Hi Mom,
>
> What's up? Just a quick note to say this really nice professor took interest in me and is helping me with my paper. You were right, this university is so right for me!

After selecting the best tone, you then **write with a specific purpose,** such as informing, entertaining, or persuading your audience:

> Dear Dr. Rowley,
>
> I cannot attend class next Tuesday because the lacrosse team has an away game. Attached is the schedule from my coach. I will find what I missed from another class member and give you Tuesday's assignment Monday night to remain on schedule.
>
> Hi Mom,
>
> Just wanted to let you know I'm doing okay with school. Things were pretty hectic at first, though I have made some friends, am working hard on my English research paper, and I think I'm starting in the lacrosse game next Tuesday. Your little girl is doing great!

The Importance of the Subject Line

If you use email frequently, you know how overwhelming your inbox gets, making the subject line a critical component of online letter writing. In 27b, *The Thomson Handbook* compares the subject line to a summary of the email, meaning your subject line quickly condenses or provides context to the reader.

Effective Subject Lines:	**Vague Subject Lines**
Need help with research	I'm lost
A quick update on school	Misc. school
Send money now!	Need help
Absence on Tuesday	Regarding class

Writing Email Body Text

How you write the body or the text of the email depends on whether you are the original or first author or whether you are responding to a note sent to you. If you are the original author, here are a few considerations:

- *Length:* always match the length of the email to the audience and purpose. If you are writing a parent, boyfriend/girlfriend, or someone far away, length matters less than when writing to someone you see all the time or someone of a more "official" nature, like a professor or classmate. However, messages written too briefly can be confusing and cryptic to even those most close to you:

  Charlie,

  Well?

  Jose

- *Imbedded images:* used mostly for fun correspondence, pictures can either enliven your email or be completely inappropriate.

Fun and appropriate:

Dear Mom,

Look at the latest member of the family! I told you he loves catching mice!

Love, Beth

Inappropriate:

Dear Dr. Schwarze,

The reason why I could not complete my homework is that my new kitten stole my mouse, ha ha!

Your student, Beth

- *Responding to a message:* typical email decorum requires you, the responder, to include the message below the most recent post. This permits the reader who may not even be the original writer to go back and read the post that prompted a reply, especially if he or she does not understand your message. Some reply within the original text, but this style is difficult to read and is not widely practiced. If you are participating in a lengthy correspondence, you may clean up the "thread" by deleting redundant copies, but that is a personal prerogative.

Creating Identity on the Internet: Listservs, Blogs, Wikis, *Facebook, MySpace, YouTube, Xanga,* and the List Goes On

Listservs or Discussion Lists

Since the World Wide Web has evolved, people have used this massive tool to find, congregate, talk, share information, and enjoy like-minded people by creating **online communities** or **social networks.** Some groups are professionally based and others cater to personal interests. Likewise, people in professional groups, especially those who have been long-term contributors or who meet at conferences and events outside of the online group, pepper their conversations with personal responses.

Your professors may ask you to become a member of professional discussion lists or they may develop class discussion lists.

Always remember that each discussion list, Web site, or portal has a set of guidelines for members. As discussed in the introduction to Chapter 27 in *The Thomson Handbook,* "netiquette" or "guides to email etiquette" (603) is a serious issue. An individual who fails to comply with a group's wishes typically gets reprimanded, and repeated failures result in being deleted from the group.

For a detailed list of expectations and requirements for discussion lists, consult pages 618–620 in *The Thomson Handbook.* Here are a few highlights:

- "Lurk" or read posts without commenting until you understand the regular participants, the tone and tenor of the list, and its purpose. After reading for a while you should feel comfortable contributing, but remember, not everyone regularly or even semi-regularly posts to the list.

- When you respond, make sure you read the entire thread to avoid asking repetitive questions or making redundant comments.

- Review the archives for issues before you post a question for information to insure that the topic has not already been covered.

- Regardless of how a response hits you, resist responding with inflammatory language called "flaming."
- Remember, the delete button is your friend.

Weblogs or Blogs

Whereas discussion lists are more professionally based, the blog, which is short for "Web log" that became one word, "Weblog," can be professional, personal, or both. Blogs are the creation of their owner and readers are subject to that individual's tastes, opinions, and rules. Though the reader has an opportunity to comment on any given posting, comments are never seen on the main page, so viewers are always presented the blog owner's thoughts first and foremost.

Whereas listservs or list discussions are community based and must observe rules for the group, many bloggers enjoy more controversial attitudes and language. Regardless of your mission and purpose, remember that your blog is to be read, not ignored, so how you treat your audience matters.

A problematic blog:

"Well here we go again. Every election, whether we vote for the local Treasurer or for the President of the United States, the public must endure crappy ads filled with whiney complaints. 'Don't vote for X because he is corrupt.' And always around election time everyone is for education and welfare. What happens after the election? No money for education or welfare. Ripped off again. That's how our politicians treat their constituents and we act like grateful dogs lapping up the occasional treat when they come to town to speak. What a bunch of baloney."

This entry reads like "stream of consciousness," a literary technique where the writer simply records the random thoughts that run through the brain without trying to tie together or blend the thoughts. Also, this appears to be nothing more than a rant in which the author is not interested in a counterpoint or even agreement—simply just blowing off steam is not enough. Blogs should encourage thinking and responding, even ask questions to elicit response.

Problematic blog revised:

"Election time is upon us and I have to wonder how many of you are like me, sick of the barrage of ads where each candidate whines and complains about the other. How about sticking to the issues for a change? The problem is that the politicians run the tenor of the campaign instead of the voters, so let's turn the tables and force these elected officials to work for our votes instead of spinning us.
Step One: require at least two debates where all candidates must participate.
Step Two: set rules about campaign advertising to require the ads to stick to the issues and leave mudslinging behind.
Step Three: Require all incumbents to post voting histories so the public can see their records. Challengers must post how they would have voted on those issues.
By working as a collective voting community without partisanism, the people will show the leaders how to lead."

The lack of inflammatory language or hostile attitude makes this response easier to read. Whereas the first response merely points out problems, this one provides solutions to which readers can react.

Creating a blog is quite simple, thanks to free blog generator software readily available on the Internet; just conduct a simple search using the terms "how to make a blog." Similar to other social networking tools, you can use your blog to sound off about issues, gather like-minded people, persuade those with views different than yours to enter the discussion, and disseminate information.

Remember, your blog and all your comments become public domain the minute you hit "Post." There have been many articles in the newspapers recently discussing how employers are finding their employees' blogs on the Internet, how employers look for job applicants' blogs, and even how the government searches for soldiers' blogs. Ultimately, you are responsible for the content in your blog.

Wikis

Wiki, which means "quick" in Hawaiian, is also a term for a collaborative blog. As you just learned, blogs are typically owned and operated by individuals, but anyone can contribute to a wiki; thus they are owned by the many writers who post on them. Popular wikis can have several thousand member/contributors, such as the online encyclopedia, *Wikipedia*.

Most reputable wikis have fact checkers, but because anyone can author a post, you should be very careful about what you consider reliable online information. Recently, the owner of *Wikipedia* claimed college students should not use the site for research. For more information, see <http://en.wikipedia.org/wiki/Wikipedia:Reliable_sources>.

Social Networking

The newest form of communication on the Internet falls under the term *social networking*, because users utilize programs to create and maintain identities on the Internet. Web sites like *Facebook, MySpace,* and *Xanga, Friendster*, and to a degree *YouTube* allow members to post personal and social information about themselves, pictures, videos, and audio files for others to access. Originally, to become a member of *Facebook*, you must be a student, but now anyone can join. The others have no special requirements.

People create profiles for a variety of reasons, such as reconnecting with old friends; making new friends; and discovering new trends by reading profiles where users list favorite movies, music, books, and quotations.

Writing and Designing Web Pages and Sites

The Internet has given every author the opportunity to publish and be read by potentially millions of people, whereas in traditional print writing people must read, judge, and accept a piece of submitted writing. The Web as everyman's information superhighway can be seen as both a positive and a negative because for every Web site with quality information, there are a dozen bogus or disreputable sites—making the quest for knowledge difficult.

Before you begin writing the text of your Web page and designing its look, here are a few concepts to consider:

- Web page writing is different from print or traditional writing.
- Studies show people read online text differently from traditional text.
- Color and image choice are secondary to text according to Web users.
- Good Web sites appeal to a small audience, whereas poor ones try to appeal to a broad audience.

Targeting Your Web Audience with Style and Structure

Like writing your papers, writing a Web page or a suite of Web pages called a Web site, you must clearly identify your **audience, purpose, style** and **sentence and paragraph structure.**

- Your **audience** must be clearly defined, because not everyone wants to read about your family's vacation in New Mexico, how to prune a crepe myrtle, or a comparison/contrast between authors Judith Ortiz Cofer and Sandra Cisneros. *The main reason why users get frustrated with the Internet today is that too many Web pages focus on broad audiences.* As Web users we are fickle people because we know that if one site does not deliver immediately, there are plenty of others that will.

- The **purpose** of your Web site must be as finely focused as possible, just like the audience. People who do not know you might love reading about your family's vacation to New Mexico if your purpose is consistent and interesting.

- One central difference between Web writing **style** and print discourse **style** is that Web pages tend to be a bit less formal in language and sentence style. *However,* **style** is dictated by purpose and audience, so if your Web site contrasts Ortiz and Cisneros, you will probably write formally.

- Your **sentence and paragraph structure** are the most different aspects of Web and traditional writing. Since studies indicate reading on the computer screen is more difficult than on the printed page and that many readers scan Web pages, you must adjust your writing by providing headings that stand out from the paragraphs, writing shorter sentences, and "frontloading" your page and paragraphs so that you feature the most important information first and work down to the most general. Consider paragraphs as "chunks" devoted to a single idea.

For example, here is a traditional print abstract Danielle Brigida wrote for her Biology lab class:

A set of twenty hand prints were used in evaluating the direct correlation between the span of the hand and the height of the individual. Measuring from the tip of the thumb to the tip of the pinkie the distance was recorded in centimeters. The results from this experiment drawn from the graph were that the relationship between height and finger span is yet to be determined. Though similarities were discovered, no data solidified the hypothesis.

Here is Danielle's abstract modified for the Web:

Abstract
To determine whether there is a direct correlation between a person's hand span and height, we measured the hands of twenty participants.

Method
We measured participants by tip of thumb to tip of pinkie and recorded the results in centimeters.

Results
The data concluded that the relationship between finger span and height cannot be determined.

Usability and Navigation

Unlike traditional paper writing, you must consider **usability, user browser/platform, navigation,** and **structure.** Also, your Web page must be **intuitive.**

- **Usability** means that your audience has no trouble seeing the page as you wrote and designed it. All links must work, the page must load easily, and your color scheme must complement and not distract or make the words difficult to read.

- Since you can never know for sure where your audience might view your page, under what circumstances, using what kind of computer, and which browser (the software that reads the html code, such as *Mozilla, Internet Explorer,* and *Netscape*), you must design with **browser/platform** concerns in mind, because each browser and each computer has different restraints, sizes, and resolutions.

- **Navigation,** or how easily your audience can travel through your links to different pages or how you link certain key words or short phrases is critical to the success of your Web page. If your links are broken, meaning they don't work, your audience will grow frustrated and leave.

- To be **intuitive** means your page must be easily readable regardless of structure, because you can never be sure where your users begin reading, especially if your audience enters your site through a page other than the "Home" page.

Text and Graphics

Visuals complete the Web package and literally define the medium by giving audiences enhancements to the text. Your color scheme, the photographs or graphic images you use, the banners, logos, and buttons you incorporate all must work together as a cohesive unit. *Remember, readers come to Web pages for information, so never subordinate your text with graphics, color, and images.*

- When choosing colors, pick contrasting or dark and light hues. Use either light text on dark backgrounds or dark text on light backgrounds for readability.

- If you create a background image, make sure it does not become too "busy" and distracting.

- Limit the number of photographs (jpgs) you have on any single page (except an album page) because these larger files slow down the loading time and can frustrate your viewers.

- Avoid motion graphics, the pictures that appear to move across the screen, as well as other moving "marquees" and motion images. They may initially look cute to the designer, but most readers find them distracting and even annoying.

- Balance your Web page so text and graphics appear symmetrical. Always anchor the page with a banner across the top to orient users. Most users expect a navigation system to appear down the left side of the page (vertical) or at the top (horizontal).

Hyperlinks define Web writing because they are found in no other medium. You can provide pictures and color in print, but giving your audience a hyperlink means you have provided them a place for additional information, which gives you the opportunity to space text out by linking key concepts on different pages. However, do not go hyperlink crazy or link more than key words:

For more, go to the Products page. Readers can find more by clicking on Products.

Level 1

Name_____ **Date**_____

DIRECTIONS Read each email scenario and provide the appropriate tone, attitude, purpose (inform, entertain, persuade), and subject line in the space below.

SAMPLE

> Jennie goes to school in Virginia and is emailing her best friend in Nebraska to update her on life and her new boyfriend, Carl.
> Tone: informal, happy, playful
> Attitude: excitement that things are going well and she has a new boyfriend
> Purpose: to entertain friend with stories about school and Carl
> Subject Line: My New Boyfriend

1. Joanna is emailing her boss because she needs Wednesday and Thursday off from work to study for her midterm.
   Tone:
   Attitude:
   Purpose:
   Subject Line:

2. Hector is emailing a fellow student whom he does not know well to get the homework for a class he missed.
   Tone:
   Attitude:
   Purpose:
   Subject Line:

3. Joel and Deidre are emailing their psychology professor with questions about a paper they are working on together.
   Tone:
   Attitude:
   Purpose:
   Subject Line:

Level 1

Name_____ **Date**_____

DIRECTIONS Read each email scenario, choose the appropriate tone and attitude, and write the text to best suit the audience and purpose.

SAMPLE

Write an email to your father asking him to let you go snow skiing in Lake Tahoe, NV during the winter break.

Tone: respectful
Attitude: responsible
Dad, I was recently invited to go snow skiing in Lake Tahoe, NV during a part of our winter break from school, and I am writing to ask you to consider financing this wonderful opportunity. I have already done the research on plane tickets and can get a great rate if I act within the next two weeks, and my friend and I would stay with his parents, so lodging will be free. Think about the possibility, look at the itinerary I attached, and I will call you on Friday.

1. It is three weeks before school starts. Write an email introducing yourself to your future roommate whom you have not yet met.
   Tone:
   Attitude:

2. Your school records were accidentally mixed with another student's who shares your same name. Write an email to the registrar's office explaining the error and asking them to correct the problem.
   Tone:
   Attitude:

3. You read an article in the local newspaper that describes people your age as lazy and incompetent. Write a response email to the editorial editor, giving your side of the issue.
   Tone:
   Attitude:

4. Your professor returned midterm exams and you disagree with the grade and the comments on your paper. Write an email requesting an appointment and explain why you want to meet.
   Tone:
   Attitude:

5. Since starting college, you have neglected personal correspondence. Pick a member of your family and write a "catch up" email.
   Tone:
   Attitude:

6. You noticed in the campus newspaper that the library has work study and regular job openings. Write an email to the Head Librarian expressing an interest in one of the positions and give reasons why you would be suitable for the job.

Tone:

Attitude:

Level 1

Name_____ Date_____

DIRECTIONS The following email discussions and blogs have problems. Read each scenario, choose the appropriate tone and attitude, and revise the response using a more effective approach.

SAMPLE

Email discussion entry:
It seems that you are all wrong in your approaches to the problem, and I can't sit on my hands any longer while you keep headed down the path of most resistance! Outdoor concerts are not dangerous when properly staffed by law enforcement, so quit being so small minded and start scheduling more outdoor shows.

Revision:
I would like to add a different view from the ones posted on this discussion regarding whether to plan more or less outdoor concerts this fall. First, concerns about fan safety are certainly important and necessary; however, if we look at Phoenix's recent shows, we can see that with enough law enforcement and concert staffing, we can adequately take care of the audience and the performers. Outdoor venues bring in lots of money and contribute to the community's culture, so I hope we work toward more opportunities for bands and acts.

1. Blog:
At this point in my life, I don't care about anyone but my boyfriend. Ryan is the greatest guy because he loves me. Love is the greatest thing because it makes you feel so strong and powerful like you could do anything. I feel like I could do anything now. If no one makes me feel like Ryan, why should I hang with anyone but him? Write me back!

_____

_____

2. Email discussion list:
When I read the homework for last night I could not help but think about the discussion, or should I say argument, Mark and I got into during class the other day. Clearly Mark believes Toni Morrison is a better author than Eudora Welty, and I feel the opposite. I challenge all of you on this list to pick a side and defend it!

_____

_____

3. Blog entry:

I just read Betty's reply to my post this morning where I say the U.S. needs to lift the export embargo on Cuba and frankly, I'm not happy. Betty, you need to understand that millions of Cubans are suffering greatly because of a couple of bigheads who can't agree on politics. They drive cars from the 1950s. Their buildings are crumbling. They are hungry. So what if Cuba is communist and the U.S. is a democracy? What does that have to do with literally starving innocent people? Geez, get a grip.

_____

_____

4. Email discussion entry:

I know you have been discussing the conference in New York City, how to register, and what to do once we get there, but could someone summarize the discussion for me?

_____

_____

Level 1

Name_____ **Date**_____

DIRECTIONS The following sentences need to be modified from print writing to Web writing. Using the suggestions found in this chapter and in 29d of *The Thomson Handbook,* revise these paragraphs by getting rid of unnecessary wording, long sentences, and confusing structures. Underline key words you would make hyperlinks to take readers to additional pages, and create bullet lists where appropriate.

SAMPLE

Welcome to my Web site! You will learn all about how to make tables out of stuff lying around your yard in no time. Here at Alonzo's Home Décor we use the simplest of designs so that even the most basic novice can soon be making yard furniture. For more information about our designs click on the design button.

Welcome to <u>Alonzo's Home Décor</u> where we teach you how to turn your junk into yard art! Go to <u>Designs</u> to learn about the different methods, materials, and plans that we use.

No experience necessary. Even a novice will feel like an expert in no time.

1. Here at Knots R Us you will learn how to tie sailor knots, the hangman's knots, and any kind of slip knot you may ever need to know. Knot tying is a lost art that only a few people still do, so become one of the few, the proud, the knot tying people of America by signing up today.

_____

_____

_____

2. If you are looking for a good deal on a used car, you have come to the right place. Here at Carr's Cars, we carry only the finest Fords, Oldsmobiles, Chevrolets, and a whole bunch of Hondas, Toyotas, and Hyundais. No deal is left undone with Carr's, so come on down for a good deal today.

_____

_____

_____

3. This past July the Mallicotte family had their first family reunion ever. We got Uncle Dick and Anita from New York, Uncle Bob and Aunt Janie from North Carolina, Mary from Virginia, Stuart from Colorado, and a whole bunch of other Mallicotte relations together. The main event was the big barbeque that was held in on Blount Point Road where lots of the family used to live, but there were also lots of other things going on too, like the Day Two tour of the Mariner's Museum, a picnic on the James River, and an evening dinner at the Peninsula Arts Museum. To see pictures, click on this link: pictures.

_____

_____

_____

4. The Outer Banks in North Carolina are a series of barrier islands. These islands protect the coastline against storms, hurricanes, and other natural disasters. That's their main job. The Outer Banks have become very populated and are a big tourist destination on the East Coast. On Nags Head there is Jockey's Ridge, a huge sand dune that people climb, hang glide off of, and do other fun and playful things. In Manteo tourists can go to see "The Lost Colony," a play about the first English settlers and the mystery behind how they disappeared after some of them had to go back to England. This play has been going on for 69 years, so it is a big tradition on the Outer Banks.

_____

_____

_____

Level 2

Name_____ Date_____

DIRECTIONS Choose three blogs to analyze for a one-week period. Throughout the week contribute by responding to a reply at least once for each blog you observe. To find blogs, go to http://blogsearch.google.com/ and search by subject matter or words (e.g., science fiction, mystery, films).

Read blog threads and analyze for:

Audience: Define the types of people the author seems to write to and who would be most likely to read this blog.

Purpose: Identify reasons why the author publishes on the Internet, such as to keep friends and family updated, report on political issues, etc.

Tone/Voice: Though entries change depending on the subject matter, define the overall tone and voice the author employs. What kind of language supports that tone/voice? How does the tone or voice change in the blog or is it static?

Style: What kinds of visuals does the author engage if any? How is the blog designed visually? What kind of style do the language and tone convey (angry, relaxed, confused, artful)?

_____

_____

_____

_____

_____

_____

_____

_____

_____

_____

_____